THE PENGUIN POETS

HUGH MACDIARMID

Hugh MacDiarmid is the pseudonym of C. M. Grieve, who was born in 1892, in Langholm. He attended school there and in Edinburgh, and afterwards planned to become a teacher but he gave up this idea in favour of journalism, which gave him scope for expression of his left-wing politics. He became converted to the Scots movement and began to revive the neglected language in his poems, which place him among the greatest of Scots poets. Awarded a Civil List Pension for his services to Scottish Literature, he has also received an honorary doctorate from Edinburgh University, the Fletcher of Saltoun Medal, and the Foyle Poetry Prize. He is one of the forty Fellows of the Modern Language Association of America, and one of the thirty members of the Speculative Society of Edinburgh. Previous books by Hugh MacDiarmid are *Collected Poems* (1962) and *Selected Essays* (1969).

HUGH MACDIARMID

Selected Poems

Selected and edited by
David Craig and John Manson

PENGUIN BOOKS

Penguin Books Ltd, Harmondsworth, Middlesex, England
Penguin Books Inc., 7110 Ambassador Road, Baltimore, Maryland 21207, U.S.A.
Penguin Books Australia Ltd, Ringwood, Victoria, Australia

—

This selection first published 1970
Copyright © C. M. Grieve, 1970

—

Made and printed in Great Britain by
Cox & Wyman Ltd,
London, Reading and Fakenham
Set in Monotype Fournier

CONTENTS

INTRODUCTION

THIS book aims to make readily available a comprehensive selection from the work of a poet who exacts attention on the same level as the accepted masters of modern poetry. MacDiarmid was working at the highest level from the early Twenties to the later Thirties. Yet nearly all the eight important volumes he published during those years – *Sangschaw*, *Penny Wheep*, *A Drunk Man Looks at the Thistle*, *To Circumjack Cencrastus*, *First Hymn to Lenin*, *Scots Unbound*, *Stony Limits*, *Second Hymn to Lenin* – were in limited or very small editions*, and only two of these were republished, in the Fifties. Two of his most sustained poems – "By Wauchopeside" and "Whuchulls" – were not collected into a volume until thirty-five years after their first publication. Other poems were not published at all. The manuscript of another fine later poem – "Bracken Hills in Autumn" – was lost until 1961; several important later poems had to be withheld from publication – in *Stony Limits* – on legal advice; the "Third Hymn to Lenin" and *In Memoriam James Joyce* were not published until 1955. Neither was MacDiarmid's poetry anthologized in a way that brought out and established the range of his key work. And when his *Collected Poems*, in an expensive American edition, appeared in 1962, a good many valuable poems were left out.

In the early Fifties, in a large Scottish city, we had to make extraordinary efforts – borrowing, combing catalogues, typing out whole books – to get to know the volumes from 1931–5. Yet these matter so much, if one is trying to familiarize oneself with MacDiarmid's most original and durable work, that thirty of the seventy-odd poems in this book have had to be taken from those years. It is as though, say, Yeats's meditative poems on art, culture, and growing old – the vein that runs from "Ancestral Houses" and "Among School Children" to "The Circus Animals' Desertion" – had simply not been there. Yet

*e.g. 788 copies of *Penny Wheep*, 350 of *Scots Unbound*.

all readers of modern poetry have Yeats's distinctive themes and music in their heads (and his work is on a thousand syllabuses). Beside these poems of Yeats's must be set MacDiarmid's most complex and fluent poems on the human struggle to rise to the full of our own nature and on the physical basis of that nature: e.g. "By Wauchopeside", "Water of Life", "Harry Semen", the "First Hymn to Lenin". Again, all readers of modern poetry have at some stage dwelt on those poems of Auden's with dates in their titles ("A Bride in the 30s", "A Summer Night, 1933", "Spain 1937") which try to reach the marrow of their epoch by taking long historical perspectives upon the immediate present. Beside these must be set MacDiarmid's ratiocinative poems – more abstract than Auden's best, yet unmistakably palpable – in which he envisages what it might be, and what it might take, to break out of the vicious circle, the waste of time and life, that makes nought of so much human experience. "Supposing a bomb were put under the whole scheme of things, what would we be after? What feelings do we want to carry through into the next epoch? What feelings will carry us through?" These radical questionings of D. H. Lawrence's* give the spirit also of MacDiarmid's most *concerned* poetry: e.g. the vein that runs from the more sustained trains of thought in *A Drunk Man Looks at the Thistle* to the hymns to Lenin, "The Seamless Garment", and "Lo! A Child is Born".

A glance will show that MacDiarmid's poetry, at least up until 1931–2, poses special problems for the reader. This is true whether he is English, Scottish, or African. We, the editors, were both brought up in the north of Scotland and one of us spoke Scots from his childhood, yet there are a good many lines in which each of the two or three key-words was unknown to us from print, let alone from speech. In this respect, in the range of his borrowing from older literatures, dictionaries, and specialized or technical sources (all reinforcing his own dialect, south-west Border Scots), MacDiarmid was in line with the other three important innovators of the Twenties and Thirties, Pound, Joyce and Eliot. He exacts like efforts from his readers and yields like fruits, in the way of multiple associa-

* *Phoenix* (1936), 520.

tions fused in the one phrase and perceptions never before acught in language. Yet clearly MacDiarmid's usage is much more consistently alien than that of the others (except for the special case of *Finnegans Wake*), and to help surmount this – to feed the new meanings into the reader's mind at the very point where the poem is impinging for the first time – we have glossed at the foot of each page all words that seemed likely to hold up the reader unused to literary or spoken Scots. Once one has got the habit of using these glosses they should not much break the circuit of one's understanding; and in any case is it not true that the effort of plumbing the full meanings of any major poetry, whatever the language, demands pauses and casts back, to focus more sharply and to let the utmost range of associations arise from each crux in the wording?

The difference in reading major poetry in Scots is that the enhancement, the finer tuning, of one's reading-power will have to be directed at taking in a variety of wordings that include items one has never seen before at all, not even in different arrangements. This is true also of Shakespeare. Many rich Shakespearean passages present about the same degree of alien usage as a rich piece of MacDiarmid, and if one has to stretch one's understanding to get the originality of "the dark backward and abysm of time", the same is true of MacDiarmid's "I' the how-dumb-deid o' the cauld hairst nicht" (see "The Eemis Stane", p 21). What happens in each case is that words used with such felicity *cooperate with each other*, so that the total understanding that arises as one gets into the phrase or the image helps any completely strange items over the threshold of intelligibility and into one's mind. One's linguistic knowledge is permanently added to. Of course there remain items, less helped by their context, that need straight translation. But clearly these will be very few compared with a wholly foreign language. If many British readers have been willing to make the effort to get Valéry or Prévert or Baudelaire in the original, it seems all the more likely that MacDiarmid will be found accessible once one has shed the expectation that whatever comes from the British Isles must be instantly intelligible. Matthew Arnold (in "The Study of Poetry") could absorb

Burns into his standard along with Chaucer and Gray and Shelley, with not a word of demur at the alien language. Readers today are surely as able to do as much for MacDiarmid's poetry – to integrate it into its proper place in their experience along with Yeats and Eliot, Pound and Auden.

July 1969   D. C.
                                               J. M.

NOTE ON THE LANGUAGE

In the glosses at the foot of each page the same word may be glossed differently in different places. Our effort has been to give, not a straight dictionary-equivalent, but an equivalent that catches as nearly as possible the imaginative nuances of the original and in a form (with effects of length and of vowel-and-consonant) as near as possible to the original, insofar as this was compatible with our own knowledge of what the Scots words can mean and with the meanings listed in the main dictionaries of the Scots language.

The following is a list of the commoner Scots words that come so often in the poems that it would have been irksome to see them glossed repeatedly:

a' all
abune above
ae, a'e, ane one
aince once
a'thing everything
auld old
aye always
cauld cold
een eyes
fegs faith! (mild oath)
frae from
gang go
  gaed went
  gane gone
gar'd made
gie give
  gie'd gave
gin if
haud hold
ilka each; every

ken know
  kent known, knew
lang long
mair more
maist most
maun must
nae no
nocht nothing
ocht anything
-ocht -ought (e.g. *thocht* = thought)
oor our
owre, ower over; too
roon 'round
sae so
sic such
sicna such a
syne then; since then
tae to; too
whaur where
yon that; those

NOTE ON THE TEXT

ALL the poems appear either chronologically by volumes (and in the order in which they came inside the volumes) or else, in the case of the eight not taken from volumes of MacDiarmid's, their place in the sequence of his development was worked out on stylistic grounds and checked with the poet.

Fourteen of the items are not in the *Collected Poems* (1962, 1967).

Although several long poems appear in excerpts, no break was ever made in the middle of a formal (metrical and/or rhyming) unit. Excerpting seems all the more justified in that a number of MacDiarmid's works (notably *A Drunk Man Looks at the Thistle*, *To Circumjack Cencrastus*, and "Ode to All Rebels") were written as loosely-joined sequences in a mixture of forms. (We would have been likely to include an excerpt from another such poem, "On a Raised Beach", from *Stony Limits*, had it not recently become easy to get in *Longer Contemporary Poems*, ed. David Wright, Penguin, 1966.)

Differences from the original printed texts are very few and are to correct evident mistakes, usually of commas and apostrophes. The one verbal change, in l. 42 of "Whuchulls" ("hide" substituted for "scho"), was made at MacDiarmid's request.

ACKNOWLEDGEMENTS

Acknowledgement is made to the following under whose imprint some of the poems in this selection first appeared:

William Blackwood & Sons; Castle Wynd Printers, Edinburgh; William Maclellan; MacGibbon & Kee; The Macmillan Company; *New Saltire*; the *Scotsman*.

from

SANGSCHAW
(1925)

The Bonnie Broukit Bairn

Mars is braw in crammasy,
Venus in a green silk goun,
The auld mune shak's her gowden feathers,
Their starry talk's a wheen o' blethers,
Nane for thee a thochtie sparin',
Earth, thou bonnie broukit bairn!
– *But greet, an' in your tears ye'll droun*
The haill clanjamfrie!

The Watergaw

Ae weet forenicht i' the yow-trummle
I saw yon antrin thing,
A watergaw wi' its chitterin' licht
Ayont the on-ding;
An' I thocht o' the last wild look ye gied
Afore ye deed!

There was nae reek i' the laverock's hoose
That nicht – an' nane i' mine;
But I hae thocht o' that foolish licht

Sangschaw song-show	*weet* wet
Broukit neglected	*forenicht* early evening
braw handsome	*yow-trummle* cold weather after
crammasy crimson	sheep-shearing
wheen o' blethers pack of nonsense	*antrin* rare
greet weep	*chitterin'* shivering
haill whole	*on-ding* onset
clanjamfrie jing-bang	*reek* smoke
Watergaw indistinct rainbow	*laverock's* lark's

Ever sin' syne;
An' I think that mebbe at last I ken
What your look meant then.

Au Clair de la Lune

For w. b.

*. . . She's yellow
An' yawps like a peany.*   ANON.

*They mix ye up wi' loony fowk,
Wha are o' stars the mense,
The madness that ye bring to me,
I wadna change't for sense.*   W. B.

1 · PRELUDE TO MOON MUSIC

Earth's littered wi' larochs o' Empires,
Muckle nations are dust.
Time'll meissle it awa', it seems,
An' smell nae must.

But wheest! – Whatna music is this,
While the win's haud their breath?
– *The Moon has a wunnerfu' finger
For the back-lill o' Death!*

2 · MOONSTRUCK

When the warl's couped soon' as a peerie
That licht-lookin' craw o' a body, the moon,
Sits on the fower cross-win's
Peerin' a' roon'.

yawps screeches
peany turkey-hen
mense pride
larochs fragments
Muckle great
meissle crumble
must bad smell

back-lill thumb-hole on bagpipe
   chanter
warl's world's
couped lapsed off
soon' sound
peerie spinning top

18

She's seen me – she's seen me – an' straucht
Loupit clean on the quick o' my hert.
The quhither o' cauld gowd's fairly
Gi'en me a stert.

An' the roarin' o' oceans noo'
Is peerieweerie to me:
Thunner's a tinklin' bell: an' Time
Whuds like a flee.

3 · THE MAN IN THE MOON

Oh, lad, I fear that yon's the sea
Where they fished for you and me,
And there, from whence we both were ta'en,
You and I shall drown again.   A. E. HOUSMAN

The moonbeams kelter i' the lift,
An' Earth, the bare auld stane,
Glitters beneath the seas o' Space,
White as a mammoth's bane.

An', lifted owre the gowden wave,
Peers a dumfoun'ered Thocht,
Wi' keethin' sicht o' a' there is,
An' bodily sicht o' nocht.

4 · THE HUNTRESS AND HER DOGS

Her luchts o' yellow hair
Flee oot ayont the storm,
Wi' mony a bonny flaught
The colour o' Cairngorm.

Loupit lighted
quhither beam
peerieweerie very faint
Whuds flits
flee fly
kelter undulate

lift sky
keethin' sicht glimpse as of salmon
    ripple
luchts locks
flaught gleam

Oot owre the thunner-wa'
She haiks her shinin' breists,
While th' oceans to her heels
Slink in like bidden beasts.

So sall Earth's howlin' mobs
Drap, lown, ahint the sang
That frae the chaos o' Thocht
In triumph braks or lang.

In the Hedge-Back

It was a wild black nicht,
But i' the hert o't we
Drave back the darkness wi' a bleeze o' licht,
Ferrer than een could see.

It was a wild black nicht,
But o' the snell air we
Kept juist eneuch to hinder the heat
Meltin' us utterly.

It was a wild black nicht,
But o' the win's roar we
Kept juist eneuch to hear oor herts beat
Owre it triumphantly.

It was a wild black nicht,
But o' the Earth we
Kept juist eneuch underneath us to ken
That a warl' used to be.

haiks trails   *snell* keen
sall shall   *eneuch* enough
lown silent   *warl'* world
Ferrer further

Crowdieknowe

Oh to be at Crowdieknowe
When the last trumpet blaws,
An' see the deid come loupin' owre
The auld grey wa's.

Muckle men wi' tousled beards
I grat at as a bairn
'll scramble frae the croodit clay
Wi' feck o' swearin'.

An' glower at God an' a' His gang
O' angels i' the lift
– Thae trashy bleezin' French-like folk
Wha gar'd them shift!

Fain the weemun-folk'll seek
To mak' them haud their row
– *Fegs, God's no blate gin he stirs up*
The men o' Crowdieknowe!

The Eemis Stane

I' the how-dumb-deid o' the cauld hairst nicht
The warl' like an eemis stane
Wags i' the lift;
An' my eerie memories fa'
Like a yowdendrift.

Like a yowdendrift so's I couldna read
The words cut oot i' the stane

loupin' jumping	*Eemis* unsteady
Muckle big	*how-dumb-deid* dead silent depth
grat cried	*cauld* cold
croodit crowded	*hairst* harvest
feck plenty	*warl'* world
lift sky	*lift* sky
Fain eagerly	*yowdendrift* blizzard
blate backward	

Had the fug o' fame
An' history's hazelraw
No' yirdit thaim.

Cophetua

Oh! The King's gane gyte,
Puir auld man, puir auld man,
An' an ashypet lassie
Is Queen o' the lan'.

Wi' a scoogie o' silk
An' a bucket o' siller
She's showin' the haill Coort
The smeddum intil her!

O Jesu Parvule

*Followis ane sang of the birth of Christ,
with the tune of Baw lu la law.* GODLY BALLATES

His mither sings to the bairnie Christ
Wi' the tune o' *Baw lu la law.*
The bonnie wee craturie lauchs in His crib
An' a' the starnies an' he are sib.
        Baw, baw, my loonikie, baw, balloo.

"Fa' owre, ma hinny, fa' owre, fa' owre,
A' body's sleepin' binna oorsels."
She's drawn Him in tae the bool o' her breist
But the byspale's nae thocht o' sleep i' the least.
        Balloo, wee mannie, balloo, balloo.

fug moss		*smeddum* mettle	
hazelraw lichen		*starnies* stars	
yirdit buried		*sib* kin	
gyte mad		*loonikie* little boy	
ashypet lassie skivvy		*Fa' owre* go to sleep	
scoogie apron		*binna* except	
siller silver		*bool* curve	
haill whole		*byspale* prodigy	

PENNY WHEEP
(1926)

Wheesht, Wheesht

Wheesht, wheesht, my foolish hert,
For weel ye ken
I widna ha'e ye stert
Auld ploys again.

It's guid to see her lie
Sae snod an' cool,
A' lust o' lovin' by –
Wheesht, wheesht, ye fule!

Somersault

I lo'e the stishie
O' Earth in space
Breengin' by
At a haliket pace.

A wecht o' hills
Gangs wallopin' owre,
Syne a whummlin' sea
Wi' a gallus glower.

The West whuds doon
Like the pigs at Gadara,
But the East's aye there
Like a sow at the farrow.

Penny Wheep Small Beer   *haliket* giddy
Wheesht hush   *whummlin'* tumbling
snod set   *gallus* reckless
stishie stir   *whuds* thuds
Breengin' hurtling

Hungry Waters

(*For a little Boy at Linlithgow*)

The auld men o' the sea
Wi' their daberlack hair
Ha'e dackered the coasts
O' the country fell sair.

They gobble owre cas'les,
Chow mountains to san';
Or lang they'll eat up
The haill o' the lan'.

Lickin' their white lips
An' yowlin' for mair,
The auld men o' the sea
Wi' their daberlack hair.

Focherty

Duncan Gibb o' Focherty's
A giant to the likes o' me,
His face is like a roarin' fire
For love o' the barley-bree.

He gangs through this and the neebrin' shire
Like a muckle rootless tree
– And here's a caber for Daith to toss
That'll gi'e his spauld a swee!

daberlack seaweed
dackered harried
fell sair very severely
yowlin' roaring
barley-bree whisky

neebrin' neighbouring
muckle girthy
spauld backbone
swee jerk

His gain was aye a wee'r man's loss
And he took my lass frae me,
An wi' mony a quean besides
He's ta'en his liberty.

I've had nae chance wi' the likes o' him
And he's tramped me underfit.
– Blaefaced afore the throne o' God
He'll get his fairin' yet.

He'll be like a bull in the sale-ring there,
And I'll lauch lood to see,
Till he looks up and canna mak' oot
Whether it's God – or me!

The Widower

Auld wife, on a nicht like this
Pitmirk and snell
It's hard for a man like me
To believe in himsel'.

A wheen nerves that hotch in the void,
And a drappie bluid,
And a buik that craves for the doonfa'
Like a guisand cude.

For Guid's sake, Jean, wauken up!
A word frae your mou'
Has knit my gantin' timbers
Thegither or noo.

wee'r lesser
quean lass
Blaefaced livid with fear
fairin' deserts
Pitmirk pitch dark
snell keen

wheen few
hotch jerk
buik body
guisand cude dry barrel
gantin' gaping
or noo before now

The Dead Liebknecht

(After the German of Rudolf Leonhardt)

His corpse owre a' the city lies
In ilka square and ilka street.
His spilt bluid floods the vera skies
And nae hoose but is darkened wi't.

The factory horns begin to blaw
Thro' a' the city, blare on blare,
The lowsin' time o' workers a',
Like emmits skailin' everywhere.

And wi' his white teeth shinin' yet
The corpse lies smilin' underfit.

Scunner

Your body derns
In its graces again
As the dreich grun' does
In the gowden grain,
And oot o' the daith
O' pride you rise
Wi' beauty yet
For a hauf-disguise.

The skinklan' stars
Are but distant dirt.
Tho' fer owre near
You are still – whiles – girt

owsin' unyoking
skailin' scattering
Scunner shudder
derns hides

dreich dull
grun' ground
skinklan 'shining

Wi' the bonnie licht
You bood ha'e tint
– And I lo'e Love
Wi' a scunner in't.

Empty Vessel

I met ayont the cairney
A lass wi' tousie hair
Singin' till a bairnie
That was nae langer there.

Wunds wi' warlds to swing
Dinna sing sae sweet,
The licht that bends owre a'thing
Is less ta'en up wi't.

from Songs for Christine
(*aetate* a year and a half)

The Bubblyjock

It's hauf like a bird and hauf like a bogle
And juist stands in the sun there and bouks.
It's a wunder its heid disna burst
The way it's aye raxin' its chouks.

Syne it twists its neck like a serpent
But canna get oot a richt note
For the bubblyjock swallowed the bagpipes
And the blether stuck in its throat.

bood should	*bouks* hiccups
tint lost	*raxin'* stretching
cairney stone-heap	*chouks* jaws
tousie tousled	*blether* windbag
Bubblyjock turkey-cock	

from

A DRUNK MAN LOOKS AT
THE THISTLE
(1926)

I amna' fou' sae muckle as tired – deid dune.
It's gey and hard wark coupin' gless for gless
Wi' Cruivie and Gilsanquhar and the like,
And I'm no' juist as bauld as aince I wes.

The elbuck fankles in the coorse o' time,
The sheckle's no' sae souple, and the thrapple
Grows deef and dour: nae langer up and doun
Gleg as a squirrel speils the Adam's apple.

Forbye, the stuffie's no' the real Mackay.
The sun's sel' aince, as sune as ye began it,
Riz in your vera saul: but what keeks in
Noo is in truth the vilest "saxpenny planet".

And as the worth's gane doun the cost has risen.
Yin canna thow the cockles o' yin's hert
Wi' oot ha'en' cauld feet noo, jalousin' what
The wife'll say (I dinna blame her fur't).

It's robbin' Peter to pey Paul at least. . . .
And a' that's Scotch aboot it is the name,
Like a' thing else ca'd Scottish nooadays
– A' destitute o' speerit juist the same.

fou' drunk	*dour* unyielding
muckle much	*Gleg* quick
deid dune dead done	*speils* climbs
gey and very	*Forbye* what's more
coupin' tilting	*Riz* rose
bauld fit	*keeks* peeks
elbuck elbow	*Yin* one
fankles fumbles	*thow* thaw
sheckle wrist	*ha'en'* having
souple supple	*jalousin'* reckoning
thrapple gullet	*ca'd* called
deef stiff	

(To prove my saul is Scots I maun begin
Wi' what's still deemed Scots and the folk expect,
And spire up syne by visible degrees
To heichts whereo' the fules ha'e never recked.

But aince I get them there I'll whummle them
And souse the craturs in the nether deeps,
– For it's nae choice, and ony man s'ud wish
To dree the goat's weird tae as weel's the sheep's!)

Heifetz in tartan, and Sir Harry Lauder!
Whaur's Isadora Duncan dancin' noo?
Is Mary Garden in Chicago still
And Duncan Grant in Paris – and me fou'?

Sic transit gloria Scotiae – a' the floo'ers
O' the Forest are wede awa'. (A blin' bird's nest
Is aiblins biggin' in the thistle tho'? . . .
And better blin' if'ts brood is like the rest!)

You canna gang to a Burns supper even
Wi'oot some wizened scrunt o' a knock-knee
Chinee turns roon to say, "Him Haggis – velly goot!"
And ten to wan the piper is a Cockney.

No' wan in fifty kens a wurd Burns wrote
But misapplied is a'body's property,
And gin there was his like alive the day
They'd be the last a kennin' haund to gi'e –

Croose London Scotties wi' their braw shirt fronts
And a' their fancy freen's, rejoicin'
That similah gatherings in Timbuctoo,
Bagdad – and Hell, nae doot – are voicin'

whummle overturn	*aiblins* perhaps
souse drench	*biggin'* building
craturs creatures	*scrunt* stump
s'ud should	*kennin'* understanding
dree suffer	*Croose* cocksure
weird fate	*braw* fine
wede faded	*freen's* friends

Burns' sentiments o' universal love,
In pidgin' English or in wild-fowl Scots,
And toastin' ane wha's nocht to them but an
Excuse for faitherin' Genius wi' *their* thochts.

A' *they've* to say was aften said afore
A lad was born in Kyle to blaw aboot.
What unco fate mak's *him* the dumpin'-grun'
For a' the sloppy rubbish they jaw oot?

Mair nonsense has been uttered in his name
Than in ony's barrin' liberty and Christ.
If this keeps spreedin' as the drink declines,
Syne turns to tea, wae's me for the *Zeitgeist!*

Rabbie, wad'st thou wert here – the warld hath need,
And Scotland mair sae, o' the likes o' thee!
The whisky that aince moved your lyre's become
A laxative for a' loquacity.

O gin they'd stegh their guts and haud their wheesht
I'd thole it, for "a man's a man", I ken,
But though the feck ha'e plenty o' the "a' that",
They're nocht but zoologically men.

I'm haverin', Rabbie, but ye understaun'
It gets my dander up to see your star
A bauble in Babel, banged like a saxpence
'Twixt Burbank's Baedeker and Bleistein's cigar.

There's nane sae ignorant but think they can
Expatiate on *you*, if on nae ither.
The sumphs ha'e ta'en you at your wurd, and, fegs!
The foziest o' them claims to be a – Brither!

unco strange	*thole* bear
jaw pour	*feck* majority
wae's me woe is me	*haverin'* blethering
wad'st would that	*sumphs* dunces
stegh glut	*foziest* thickest
haud their wheesht hold their tongues	

Syne "Here's the cheenge" – the star o' Rabbie Burns.
Sma' cheenge, "Twinkle, Twinkle". The memory slips
As G. K. Chesterton heaves up to gi'e
"The Immortal Memory" in a huge eclipse,

Or somebody else as famous if less fat.
You left the like in Embro in a scunner
To booze wi' thieveless cronies sic as me.
I'se warrant you'd shy clear o' a' the hunner

Odd Burns Clubs tae, or ninety-nine o' them,
And haud your birthday in a different kip
Whaur your name isna ta'en in vain – as Christ
Gied a' Jerusalem's Pharisees the slip,

– Christ wha'd ha'e been Chief Rabbi gin he'd lik't! –
Wi' publicans and sinners to foregather,
But, losh! the publicans noo are Pharisees,
And I'm no' shair o' maist the sinners either.

But that's aside the point! I've got fair waun'ert.
It's no' that I'm sae fou' as juist deid dune,
And dinna ken as muckle's whaur I am
Or hoo I've come to sprawl here 'neth the mune.

That's it! It isna me that's fou' at a',
But the fu' mune, the doited jade, that's led
Me fer agley, or 'mogrified the warld.
– For a' I ken I'm safe in my ain bed.

Jean! Jean! Gin *she's* no' here it's no' *oor* bed,
Or else I'm dreamin' deep and canna wauken,
But it's a fell queer dream if this is no'
A real hillside – and thae things thistles and bracken!

Embro Edinburgh	*fair waun'ert* clean astray
scunner loathing	*muckle's* much as
thieveless useless	*fou'* drunk
I'se I'll	*doited jade* crazy hussy
kip whorehouse	*agley* astray
losh Lord!	*fell* very
shair sure	*thae* these

It's hard wark haudin' by a thocht worth ha'en'
And harder speakin't, and no' for ilka man;
Maist Thocht's like whisky – a thoosan' under proof,
And a sair price is pitten on't even than.

As Kirks wi' Christianity ha'e dune,
Burns Clubs wi' Burns – wi' a' thing it's the same,
The core o' ocht is only for the few,
Scorned by the mony, thrang wi'ts empty name.

And a' the names in History mean nocht
To maist folk but "ideas o' their ain",
The vera opposite o' onything
The Deid 'ud awn gin they cam' back again.

A greater Christ, a greater Burns, may come.
The maist they'll dae is to gi'e bigger pegs
To folly and conceit to hank their rubbish on.
They'll cheenge folks' talk but no' their natures, fegs!

I must feed frae the common trough ana'
Whaur a' the lees o' hope are jumbled up;
While centuries like pigs are slorpin' owre't
Sall my wee 'oor be cryin': "Let pass this cup?"

In wi' your gruntle then, puir wheengin' saul,
Lap up the ugsome aidle wi' the lave,
What gin it's your ain vomit that you swill
And frae Life's gantin' and unfaddomed grave?

haudin' holding	*Sall* shall
thocht thought	*'oor* hour
ha'en' having	*gruntle* snout
sair dear	*puir wheengin'* poor whining
pitten put	*ugsome aidle* foul slop
thrang wi' full of	*lave* rest
'ud awn would own	*gantin'* gaping
ana' too	*unfaddomed* unfathomed
slorpin' guzzling	

I doot I'm geylies mixed, like Life itsel',
But I was never ane that thocht to pit
An ocean in a mutchkin. As the haill's
Mair than the pairt sae I than reason yet.

I dinna haud the warld's end in my heid
As maist folk think they dae; nor filter truth
In fishy gills through which its tides may poor
For ony *animalculae* forsooth.

I lauch to see my crazy little brain
– And ither folks' – tak'n itsel' seriously,
And in a sudden lowe o' fun my saul
Blinks dozent as the owl I ken't to be.

I'll ha'e nae hauf-way hoose, but aye be whaur
Extremes meet – it's the only way I ken
To dodge the curst conceit o' bein' richt
That damns the vast majority o' men.

I'll bury nae heid like an ostrich's,
Nor yet believe my een and naething else.
My senses may advise me, but I'll be
Mysel' nae maitter what they tell's . . .

I ha'e nae doot some foreign philosopher
Has wrocht a system oot to justify
A' this: but I'm a Scot wha blin'ly follows
Auld Scottish instincts, and I winna try.

For I've nae faith in ocht I can explain,
And stert whaur the philosophers leave aff,
Content to glimpse its loops I dinna ettle
To land the sea serpent's sel' wi' ony gaff.

geylies very much	*lowe* flame
mutchkin bottle	*dozent* dazed
haill's whole is	*wrocht* worked
poor pour	*ettle* hanker

Like staundin' water in a pocket o'
Impervious clay I pray I'll never be,
Cut aff and self-sufficient, but let reenge
Heichts o' the lift and benmaist deeps o' sea.

Water! Water! There was owre muckle o't
In yonder whisky, sae I'm in deep water
(And gin I could wun hame I'd be in het,
For even Jean maun natter, natter, natter) . . .

And in the toon that I belang tae
— What tho't's Montrose or Nazareth? —
Helplessly the folk continue
To lead their livin' death! . . .

*At darknin' hings abune the howff
A weet and wild and eisenin' air.
Spring's spirit wi' its waesome sough
Rules owre the drucken stramash there.

And heich abune the vennel's pokiness,
Whaur a' the white-weshed cottons lie;
The Inn's sign blinters in the mochiness,
And lood and shrill the bairnies cry.

The hauflins 'yont the burgh boonds
Gang ilka nicht, and a' the same,
Their bonnets cocked; their bluid that stounds
Is playin' at a fine auld game.

*From the Russian of Alexander Blok.

reenge range
lift sky
benmaist furthest
owre muckle too much
wun win
darknin' dusk
abune above
howff pub
eisenin' lustful
waesome sough lonely sigh

drucken stramash drunken rumpus
heich high
blinters glimmers
mochiness thickness
bairnies kids
hauflins teenagers
boonds boundary
bluid blood
stounds throbs

34

And on the lochan there, hauf-herted
Wee screams and creakin' oar-locks soon',
And in the lift, heich, hauf-averted,
The mune looks owre the yirdly roon'.

And ilka evenin', derf and serious
(Jean ettles nocht o' this, puir lass),
In liquor, raw yet still mysterious,
A'e freend's aye mirrored in my glass.

Ahint the sheenin' coonter gruff
Thrang barmen ding the tumblers doun.
"In vino veritas" cry rough
And reid-een'd fules that in it droon.

But ilka evenin' fey and fremt
(Is it a dream nae wauk'nin' proves?)
As to a trystin'-place undreamt,
A silken leddy darkly moves.

Slow gangs she by the drunken anes,
And lanely by the winnock sits;
Frae'r robes, atour the sunken anes,
A rooky dwamin' perfume flits.

lochan little loch	*reid-een'd* red-eyed
hauf-herted half-hearted	*fey* strange
soon' sound	*fremt* friendless
lift sky	*wauk'nin'* wakening
yirdly roon', earthly round	*trystin'* meeting
derf silent	*winnock* window
ettles guesses	*Frae'r* from her
Ahint behind	*atour* over
Thrang busy	*rooky* misty
ding bang	*dwamin'* overpowering

Her gleamin' silks, the taperin'
O' her ringed fingers, and her feathers
Move dimly like a dream wi'in,
While endless faith aboot them gethers.

I seek, in this captivity,
To pierce the veils that darklin' fa'
— See white clints slidin' to the sea,
And hear the horns o' Elfland blaw.

I ha'e dark secrets' turns and twists,
A sun is gi'en to me to haud,
The whisky in my bluid insists,
And spiers my benmaist history, lad.

And owre my brain the flitterin'
O' the dim feathers gangs aince mair,
And, faddomless, the dark blue glitterin'
O' twa een in the ocean there.

My soul stores up this wealth unspent,
The key is safe and nane's but mine.
You're richt, auld drunk impenitent,
I ken it tae — the truth's in wine!

*

*A shameless thing, for ilka vileness able,
It is deid grey as dust, the dust o' a man.
I perish o' a nearness I canna win awa' frae,
Its deidly coils aboot my buik are thrawn.

'Adapted from the Russian of Zinaida Hippius.

clints cliffs	faddomless fathomless
spiers questions	win get
benmaist inmost	buik body

36

A shaggy poulp, embracin' me and stingin',
And as a serpent cauld agen' my hert.
Its scales are poisoned shafts that jag me to the quick
— And waur than them's my scunner's fearfu' smert!

O that its prickles were a knife indeed,
But it is thowless, flabby, dowf, and numb.
Sae sluggishly it drains my benmaist life
A dozent dragon, dreidfu', deef, and dumb.

In mum obscurity it twines its obstinate rings
And hings caressin'ly, its purpose whole;
And this deid thing, whale-white obscenity,
This horror that I writhe in — is my soul!

Is it the munelicht or a leprosy
That spreids aboot me; and a thistle
Or my ain skeleton through wha's bare banes
A fiendish wund's begood to whistle?

The devil's lauchter has a *hwll* like this.
My face has flown open like a lid
— And gibberin' on the hillside there
Is a' humanity sae lang has hid! . . .

My harns are seaweed — when the tide is in
They swall like blethers and in comfort float,
But when the tide is oot they lie like gealed
And runkled auld bluid-vessels in a knot!

The munelicht ebbs and flows and wi't my thocht,
Noo movin' mellow and noo lourd and rough.
I ken what I am like in Life and Daith,
But Life and Daith for nae man are enough . . .

agen' against		*dozent* dazed	
waur worse		*begood* begun	
scunner loathing		*harns* brains	
thowless spineless		*blethers* bladders	
dowf dull		*runkled* twisted	
benmaist inmost		*lourd* heavy	

And O! to think that there are members o'
St Andrew's Societies sleepin' soon',
Wha to the papers wrote afore they bedded
On regimental buttons or buckled shoon,

Or use o' England whaur the U.K.'s meent,
Or this or that anent the Blue Saltire,
Recruitin', pedigrees, and Gude kens what,
Filled wi' a proper patriotic fire!

Wad I were them – they've chosen a better pairt,
The couthie craturs, than the ane I've ta'en,
Tyauvin' wi' this root-hewn Scottis soul;
A fer, fer better pairt – except for men.

Nae doot they're sober, as a Scot ne'er was,
Each tethered to a punctual-snorin' missus,
Whilst I, puir fule, owre continents unkent
And wine-dark oceans waunder like Ulysses. . . .

*The Mune sits on my bed the nicht unsocht,
And mak's my soul obedient to her will;
And in the dumb-deid, still as dreams are still,
Her pupils narraw to bricht threids that thrill
Aboot the sensuous windin's o' her thocht.

But ilka windin' has its coonter-pairt
– The opposite'thoot which it couldna be –
In some wild kink or queer perversity
O' this great thistle, green wi' jealousy,
That breenges'twixt the munelicht and my hert. . . .

*Suggested by the German of Else Lasker-Schüler.

soon' soundly	Tyauvin' wrestling
shoon shoes	root-hewn obstinate
anent about	unkent uncharted
Gude God	unsocht unsought
Wad would	dumb-deid dead of night
couthie craturs familiar	'thoot without
(derogatory) folk	breenges plunges

*

I wish I kent the physical basis
O' a' life's seemin' airs and graces.

It's queer the thochts a kittled cull
Can lowse or splairgin' glit annul.

Man's spreit is wi' his ingangs twined
In ways that he can ne'er unwind.

A wumman whiles a bawaw gi'es
That clean abaws him gin he sees.

Or wi' a movement o' a leg
Shows'm his mind is juist a geg.

I'se warrant Jean 'ud no' be lang
In findin' whence this thistle sprang.

Mebbe it's juist because I'm no'
Beddit wi' her that gars it grow! . . .

*A luvin' wumman is a licht
That shows a man his waefu' plicht,
Bleezin' steady on ilka bane,
Wrigglin' sinnen and twinin' vein,
Or fleerin' quick and gane again,
And the mair scunnersome the sicht
The mair for love and licht he's fain
Till clear and chitterin' and nesh
Move a' the miseries o' his flesh . . .

*Suggested by the French of Edmond Rocher.

kittled cull fondled ball	*waefu'* woeful
lowse free	*sinnen* sinew
splairgin' glit spurting sperm	*fleerin'* blazing
spreit mind	*scunnersome* sickening
ingangs innards	*fain* eager
bawaw scornful look	*chitterin'* quivering
abaws confounds	*nesh* thin-skinned
geg trick	

O lass, what see'st me
As I daur hardly see,
I marvel that your bonny een
Are as they hadna' seen.

Through a' my self-respect
They see the truth abject
   – Gin you could pierce their blindin' licht
   You'd see a fouler sicht! ...

O wha's the bride that cairries the bunch
O' thistles blinterin' white?
Her cuckold bridegroom little dreids
What he sall ken this nicht.

For closer than gudeman can come
And closer to'r than hersel',
Wha didna need her maidenheid
Has wrocht his purpose fell.

O wha's been here afore me, lass,
And hoo did he get in?
   – A man that deed or I was born
   This evil thing has din.

And left, as it were on a corpse,
Your maidenheid to me?
   – Nae lass, gudeman, sin' Time began
   'S hed ony mair to gi'e.

   But I can gi'e ye kindness, lad,
   And a pair o' willin' hands,
   And you sall ha'e my breists like stars,
   My limbs like willow wands,

daur dare	*wrocht* worked
blinterin' shining	*fell* dire
gudeman husband	

And on my lips ye'll heed nae mair,
And in my hair forget,
The seed o' a' the men that in
My virgin womb ha'e met....

Millions o' wimmen bring forth in pain
Millions o' bairns that are no' worth ha'en.

Wull ever a wumman be big again
Wi's muckle's a Christ? Yech, there's nae sayin'.

Gin that's the best that you ha'e comin',
Fegs but I'm sorry for you, wumman!

Yet a'e thing's certain – Your faith is great.
Whatever happens, you'll no' be blate! ...

Mary lay in jizzen
As it were claith o' gowd,
But it's in orra duds
Ilka ither bairntime's row'd.

Christ had never toothick,
Christ was never seeck,
But Man's a fiky bairn
Wi' bellythraw, ripples, and worm-i'-the-cheek! ...

*

O Scotland is
THE barren fig.
Up, carles, up
And roond it jig.

muckle's much as	*fiky* troublesome
no' be blate not hang back	*bellythraw* gripe
jizzen childbed	*ripples* diarrhoea
claith o' gowd cloth of gold	*worm-i'-the-cheek* toothache
orra duds odd clothes	*carles* boys
bairntime's row'd childbearing	
time's clad	

Auld Moses took
A dry stick and
Instantly it
Floo'ered in his hand.

Pu' Scotland up,
And wha can say
It winna bud
And blossom tae.

A miracle's
Oor only chance.
Up, carles, up
And let us dance!

*

Grey sand is churnin' in my lugs
The munelicht flets, and gantin' there
The grave o' a' mankind's laid bare
– On Hell itsel' the drawback rugs!

Nae man can ken his hert until
The tide o' life uncovers it,
And horror-struck he sees a pit
Returnin' life can never fill! . . .

*

The munelicht that owre clear defines
The thistle's shrill cantankerous lines
E'en noo whiles insubstantialises
Its grisly form and 'stead devises
A maze o' licht, a siller-frame,
As 'twere God's dream frae which it came,
Ne'er into bein' coorsened yet,
The essence lowin' pure in it,

lugs ears	*owre clear* too clearly
flets flits	*siller* silver
gantin' gaping	*lowin'* blazing
rugs rives	

As tho' the fire owrecam' the clay,
And left its wraith in endless day.

These are the moments when a' sense
Like mist is vanished and intense,
Magic emerges frae the dense
Body o' bein' and beeks immense
As, like a ghinn oot o' a bottle,
Daith rises frae's when oor lives crottle.

These are the moments when my sang
Clears its white feet frae oot amang
My broken thocht, and moves as free
As souls frae bodies when they dee.
There's naething left o' me ava'
Save a' I'd hoped micht whiles befa'.

Sic sang to men is little worth.
It has nae message for the earth.
Men see their warld turned tapsalteerie,
Drookit in a licht owre eerie,
Or sent birlin' like a peerie –
Syne it turns a' they've kent till then
To shapes they can nae langer ken.

Men canna look on nakit licht.
It flings them back wi' darkened sicht,
And een that canna look at it,
Maun draw earth closer roond them yet
Or, their sicht tint, find nocht insteed
That answers to their waefu' need.

And yet this essence frae the clay
In dooble form aye braks away,
For, in addition to the licht,
There is an e'er-increasin' nicht,

beeks basks	*birlin'* spinning
crottle crumble	*peerie* top
tapsalteerie topsy-turvy	*tint* lost
Drookit drenched	*waefu'* woeful

A nicht that is the bigger, and
Gangs roonds licht like an airn band
That noo and then mair tichtly grips,
And snuffs it in a black eclipse,
But rings it maistly as a brough
The mune, till it's juist bricht enough –
O wull I never lowse a licht
I canna dowse again in spite,
Or dull to haud within my sicht?

The thistle canna vanish quite.
Inside a' licht its shape maun glint,
A spirit wi' a skeleton in't.

The world, the flesh, 'll bide in us
As in the fire the unburnt buss,
Or as frae sire to son we gang
And coontless corpses in us thrang.

And e'en the glory that descends
I kenna whence on *me* depends,
And shapes itsel' to what is left
Whaur I o' me ha'e me bereft,
And still the form is mine, altho'
A force to which I ne'er could grow
Is movin' in't as 'twere a sea
That lang syne drooned the last o' me
– That drooned afore the warld began
A' that could ever come frae Man.

And as at sicna times am I,
I wad ha'e Scotland to my eye
Until I saw a timeless flame
Tak' Auchtermuchty for a name,

airn iron	*thrang* crowd
brough halo	*kenna* know not
licht spark	*sicna* such
dowse snuff	*wad* would
buss bush	

And kent that Ecclefechan stood
As pairt o' an eternal mood.

Ahint the glory comes the nicht
As Maori to London's ruins,
And I'm amused to see the plicht
O' Licht as't in the black tide droons,
Yet even in the brain o' Chaos
For Scotland I wad hain a place,
And let Tighnabruaich still
Be pairt and paircel o' its will,
And Culloden, black as Hell,
A knowledge it has o' itsel'.

Thou, Dostoevski, understood,
Wha had your ain land in your **bluid**,
And into it as in a mould
The passion o' your bein' rolled,
Inherited in turn frae Heaven
Or sources fer abune it even.

Sae God retracts in endless stage
Through angel, devil, age on age,
Until at last his infinite natur'
Walks on earth a human cratur'
(Or less than human as to my een
The people are in Aiberdeen);
Sae man returns in endless growth
Till God in him again has scouth.

For sic a loup towards wisdom's croon
Hoo fer a man maun base him doon,
Hoo plunge aboot in Chaos ere
He finds his needfu' fittin' there,
The matrix oot o' which sublime
Serenity sall soar in time!

hain keep	*scouth* scope
fer abune far above	*loup* leap

Ha'e I the cruelty I need,
Contempt and syne contempt o' that,
And still contempt in endless meed
That I may never yet be caught
In ony satisfaction, or
Bird-lime that winna let me soar?

Is Scotland big enough to be
A symbol o' that force in me,
In wha's divine inebriety
A sicht abune contempt I'll see?

For a' that's Scottish is in me,
As a' things Russian were in thee,
And I in turn 'ud be an action
To pit in a concrete abstraction
My country's contrair qualities,
And mak' a unity o' these
Till my love owre its history dwells,
As owretone to a peal o' bells.

And in this heicher stratosphere
As bairn at giant at thee I peer. . . .

*

The wan leafs shak' atour us like the snaw.
Here is the cavaburd in which Earth's tint.
There's naebody but Oblivion and us,
Puir gangrel buddies, waunderin' hameless in't.

The stars are larochs o' auld cottages,
And a' Time's glen is fu' o' blinnin' stew.
Nae freen'ly lozen skimmers: and the wund
*Rises and separates even me and you.**

* Dostoevski

meed measure	*gangrel buddies* tramping folk
winna won't	*larochs* fragments
heicher higher	*blinnin' stew* blinding drift
atour above	*lozen* windowpane
cavaburd blizzard	*skimmers* flickers
tint lost	

I ken nae Russian and you ken nae Scots.
We canna tell oor voices frae the wund.
The snaw is seekin' everywhere: oor herts
At last like roofless ingles it has f'und.

And gethers there in drift on endless drift,
Oor broken herts that it can never fill;
And still – its leafs like snaw, its growth like wund –
The thistle rises and forever will . . !

*

The stars like thistle's roses floo'er
The sterile growth o' Space ootour,
That clad in bitter blasts spreids oot
Frae me, the sustenance o' its root.

O fain I'd keep my hert entire,
Fain hain the licht o' my desire,
But ech! the shinin' streams ascend,
And leave me empty at the end.

For aince it's toomed my heart and brain,
The thistle needs maun fa' again.
– But a' its growth 'll never fill
The hole it's turned my life intill! . . .

Yet ha'e I Silence left, the croon o' a'.

No' her, wha on the hills langsyne I saw
Liftin' a foreheid o' perpetual snaw.

No' her, wha in the how-dumb-deid o' nicht
Kyths, like Eternity in Time's despite.

No' her, withooten shape, wha's name is Daith,
No' Him, unkennable abies to faith

ootour across	*how-dumb-deid* dead silent depth
fain gladly	*Kyths* appears
hain keep	*unkennable* unknowable
toomed emptied	*abies* except
langsyne long ago	

– God whom, gin e'er He saw a man, 'ud be
E'en mair dumfooner'd at the sicht than he.

– But Him, whom nocht in man or Deity,
Or Daith or Dreid or Laneliness can touch,
Wha's deed owre often and has seen owre much.

O I ha'e Silence left,

      – "And weel ye micht,"
Sae Jean'll say, "efter sic a nicht!"

from

TO CIRCUMJACK CENCRASTUS

(1930)

*

Hunters were oot on a Scottish hill
A'e day when the sun stude suddenly still
At noon and turned the colour o' port,
A perfect nuisance, spoilin' their sport.
Syne it gaed pitch black a'thegither.
Isn't that juist like oor Scottish weather!

*

Lourd on my hert as winter lies
The state that Scotland's in the day.
Spring to the North has aye come slow
But noo dour winter's like to stay
      For guid,
      And no' for guid!

dumfooner'd dumbfounded   *Cencrastus* serpent
Circumjack encompass   *Lourd* leaden

O wae's me on the weary days
When it is scarce grey licht at noon;
It maun be a' the stupid folk
Diffusin' their dullness roon and roon
                Like soot,
                That keeps the sunlicht oot.

Nae wonder if I think I see
A lichter shadow than the neist
I'm fain to cry: "The dawn, the dawn!
I see it brakin' in the East."
                But ah
                — It's juist mair snaw!

                        *

I wha aince in Heaven's height
Gethered to me a' the licht
Can nae mair reply to fire,
'Neth deid leafs buriet in the mire.

Sib to dewdrop, rainbow, ocean,
No' for me their hues and motion.
This foul clay has filed me till
It's no' to ken I'm water still.

                        *

North of the Tweed

Cauld licht and tumblin' cloods. It's queer
There's never been a poet here . . .

Shades o' the Sun-King no' yet risen
Are sleepin' in a corner on the straw.
Despair seems to touch bottom time and again
But aye Earth opens and reveals fresh depths.

wae's woe is   *sib* kin
neist next   *filed* dirtied

49

The pale-wa'd warld is fu' o' licht and life
Like a glass in which water faintly stirs.
Gie owre a' this tomfoolery, and sing
The movin' spirit that nae metaphor drawn
Frae water or frae licht can dim suggest.
Leid in nae mere Longinian hypsos come
But in inhuman splendours, triumphin' wi'
"A dazzlin' disregard o' the soul."
                    Nocht else 'll dae.

Water nor licht nor yet the barley field
That shak's in silken sheets at ilka braith,
Its lang nap thrawin' the quick licht aboot
In sic a maze that tak's and gies at aince
As fair oot-tops the coontless ripplin' sea.
There's nae chameleon like the July fields;
Their different colours change frae day to day
While they shift instantly neath the shiftin' licht
Yet they're owre dull for this, stagnant and dull;
And even your een, beloved, and your hair
Are like the barley and the sea and Heaven
That flaw and fail and are defeated by
                    The blind turns o' chance.

Thinkna' that I'm ungratefu', wi' nae mind
O' Deirdre and the fauld o' sunbeams* yet,
Or canna find on bracken slopes abune the bog
The orchis smellin' like cherry-pie;
Or that the sun's blade cuttin' straightly through
A cloudy sea fails wi' my cloudy hert,
Releasin' it frae self-disgust until I tine
A' sense o' livin' under set conditions
And live in an unconditioned space o' time

        *"Fold of sunbeams" – Glendaruel.

        wa'd walled   fauld fold
        Gie owre leave off   tine lose
        Leid language

Perfect in ilka pulse and impulse, and aince mair
A seven-whistler in Kintyre, or yon broon hill
That's barren save for fower pale violets on
             A South-leanin' bank.

I've sat amang the crimson buds o' thrift
Abune the sea whaur Buachaille herds the waves;
And seen the primrose nightglow to the North
Owre Moray and the flat sea while the West
Still held a twinkle o' the morning-star,
(For in the Cairngorms simmer nicht and dawn
Come close, but canna thraw the larks' hours oot);
And hoo should I forget the Langfall
On mornings when the hines were ripe but een
Ahint the glintin' leafs were brichter still
Than sunned dew on them, lips reider than the fruit,
And I filled baith my basket and my hert
             Mony and mony a time?

And yet you mind, dear, on the bridal hill
Hoo yon laich loch ootshone my een in yours,
Nor wi' the heather could oor bluid compete,
Nor could the ring I gi'ed you when your hand
Lay on the crucifers compare wi' them
Save for a second when the sun seized on't.
Hair of the purple of Strathendrick Hill,
Slant e'en wi' pupils like blue-stane washed wi' rain
And the whites owre white and the hunted look.
Here tak' your bairn; I've cairried it lang eneuch,
Langer than maist men wad, as weel you ken.
Noo I'll pipe insteed – what tune'll you hae? –
             On Rudha nam Marbh.*

*

*"The **Point** of the Dead."

fower four	*mind* remember
hines raspberries	*laich* low(-lying)

To hell wi' happiness!
I sing the terrifying discipline
O' the free mind that gars a man
Mak' his joys kill his joys,
The weakest by the strongest,
The temporal by the fundamental
(Or hope o' the fundamental)
And prolong wi'in himself
Threids o' thocht sae fragile
It needs the help and contrivance
O' a' his vital poo'er
To haud them frae brakin'
As he pu's them owre the gulfs.
Oor humanity canna follow us
To lichts sae faur removed.
A man ceases to be himsel'
Under sicna constraint.
Will he find life or daith
At the end o' his will,
At Thocht's deepest depth,
Or some frichtfu' sensation o' seein'
Nocht but the ghastly glimmer
O' his ain puir maitter?
                What does it maitter?
                It's the only road.
The beaten track is *beaten* frae the stert.

*

  gars forces   *pu's* pulls

FIRST HYMN TO LENIN
AND OTHER POEMS
(1931)

First Hymn to Lenin

To Prince D. S. Mirsky

Few even o' the criminals, cravens, and fools
Wha's voices vilify a man they ken
They've cause to fear and are unfit to judge
As they're to stem his influence again
But in the hollows where their herts should be
                    Foresee your victory.

Churchills, Locker-Lampsons, Beaverbrooks'll be
In history's perspective less to you
(And them!) than the Centurions to Christ
Of whom, as you, at least this muckle's true
– "Tho' pairtly wrang he cam' to richt amang's
                    Faur greater wrangs."

Christ's cited no' by chance or juist because
You mark the greatest turnin'-point since him
But that your main redress has lain where he's
Least use – fulfillin' his sayin' lang kept dim
That whasae followed him things o' like natur'
                    'Ud dae – and greater!

Certes nae ither, if no' you's dune this.
It maitters little. What you've dune's the thing,
No' hoo't compares, corrects, or complements
The work of Christ that's taen owre lang to bring
Sic a successor to keep the reference back
                    Natural to mak'.

muckle's much is   *whasae* whoever

Great things ha'e aye ta'en great men in the past
In some proportion to the work they did,
But you alane to what you've dune are nocht
Even as the poo'ers to greater ends are hid
In what's ca'd God, or in the common man,
                    Withoot your plan.

Descendant o' the unkent Bards wha made
Sang peerless through a' post-anonymous days
I glimpse again in you that mightier poo'er
Than fashes wi' the laurels and the bays
But kens that it is shared by ilka man
                    Since time began.

Great things, great men – but at faur greater's cost!
If first things first had had their richtfu' sway
Life and Thocht's misused poo'er might ha' been ane
For a' men's benefit – as still they may
Noo that through you this mair than elemental force
                    Has f'und a clearer course.

Christ said: "Save ye become as bairns again."
Bairnly eneuch the feck o' us ha' been!
Your work needs men; and its worst foes are juist
The traitors wha through a' history ha' gi'en
The dope that's gar'd the mass o' folk pay heed
                    And bide bairns indeed.

As necessary, and insignificant, as death
Wi' a' its agonies in the cosmos still
The Cheka's horrors are in their degree;
And'll end suner! What maitters 't wha we kill
To lessen that foulest murder that deprives
                    Maist men o' real lives?

fashes bothers   *feck* majority

For now in the flower and iron of the truth
To you we turn; and turn in vain nae mair,
Ilka fool has folly eneuch for sadness
But at last we are wise and wi' laughter tear
The veil of being, and are face to face
          Wi' the human race.

Here lies your secret, O Lenin, – yours and oors,
No' in the majority will that accepts the result
But in the real will that bides its time and kens
The benmaist resolve is the poo'er in which we exult
Since naebody's willingly deprived o' the good;
          And, least o' a', the crood!

At My Father's Grave

The sunlicht still on me, you row'd in clood,
We look upon each ither noo like hills
Across a valley. I'm nae mair your son.
It is my mind, nae son o' yours, that looks,
And the great darkness o' your death comes up
And equals it across the way.
A livin' man upon a deid man thinks
And ony sma'er thocht's impossible.

Prayer for a Second Flood

There'd ha'e to be nae warnin'. Times ha'e changed
And Noahs are owre numerous nooadays,
(And them the vera folk to benefit maist!)
Knock the feet frae under them, O Lord, wha praise
Your unsearchable ways sae muckle and yet hope
          To keep within knowledgeable scope!

bides waits	*row'd* wrapped
benmaist inmost	*muckle* much
sma'er smaller	

Ding a' their trumpery show to blauds again.
Their measure is the thimblefu' o' Esk in spate.
Like whisky the tittlin' craturs mete oot your poo'ers
Aince a week for bawbees in the kirk-door plate,
— And pit their umbrellas up when they come oot
     If mair than a pulpitfu' o' You's aboot!

O arselins wi' them! Whummle them again!
Coup them heels-owre-gowdy in a storm sae gundy
That mony a lang fog-theekit face I ken
'll be sooked richt doon under through a cundy
In the High Street, afore you get weel-sterted
     And are still hauf-herted!

Then flush the world in earnest. Let yoursel' gang,
Scour't to the bones, and mak' its marrow holes
Toom as a whistle as they used to be
In days I mind o' ere men fidged wi' souls,
But naething had forgotten you as yet,
     Nor you forgotten it.

Up then and at them, ye Gairds o' Heaven,
The Divine Retreat is owre. Like a tidal bore
Boil in among them; let the lang lugs nourished
On the milk o' the word at last hear the roar
O' human shingle; and replenish the salt o' the earth
     In the place o' their birth.

ding smash	*heels-owre-gowdy* head over heels
blauds pieces	*gundy* ravenous
tittlin' whispering	*fog-theekit* moss-thatched
bawbees ha'pennies	*cundy* conduit
arselins on their arse	*Toom* clean
Whummle tumble	*fidged* itched
Coup upend	*lugs* ears

Charisma and My Relatives
To William McElroy

No' here the beloved group; I've gane sae faur
(Like Christ) yont faither, mither, brither, kin
I micht as weel try dogs or cats as seek
In sic relationships again to fin'
The epopteia I maun ha'e – and feel
    (Frae elsewhere) owre me steal.

But naewhere has the love-religion had
A harder struggle than in Scotland here
Which means we've been untrue as fechters even
To oor essential genius – Scots, yet sweer
To fecht in, or owre blin' to see where lay,
    The hert o' the fray.

We've focht in a' the sham fechts o' the world.
But I'm a Borderer and at last in me
The spirit o' my people's no' content
Wi' ony but the greatest enemy,
And nae mair plays at sodgers but has won
    To a live battle-grun'.

A fiercer struggle than joukin' it's involved.
Oorsels oor greatest foes. Yet, even yet,
I haud to "I" and "Scot" and "Borderer"
And fence the wondrous fire that in me's lit
Wi' sicna barriers roond as hide frae'ts licht
    Near a'body's sicht.

And cry "as weel try dogs or cats as seek
In sic relationships again to fin'
The epopteia" that, yet f'und, like rain

fechters fighters   *joukin'* dodging
sweer loth

57

'Ud quickly to the roots o' a' thing rin
Even as the circles frae a stane that's hurled
    In water ring the world.

Sae to my bosom yet a' beasts maun come,
Or I to theirs, – baudrons, wi' sides like harps,
Lookin' like the feel o' olives in the mooth,
Yon scabby cur at whom the gutter carps,
Nose-double o' the taste o' beer-and-gin,
    And a' my kin.

And yet – there's some folk lice'll no' live on,
I'm ane o' them I doot. But what a thocht!
What speculations maun a man sae shunned
No' ha'e until at last the reason's brocht
To view acceptable, as the fact may be
    On different grun's to them and me.

The Seamless Garment

Whene'er the mist which stands 'twixt God and thee
Defecates to a pure transparency   COLERIDGE

    You are a cousin of mine
      Here in the mill.
    It's queer that born in the Langholm
      It's no' until
    Juist noo I see what it means
    To work in the mill like my freen's.

    I was tryin' to say something
      In a recent poem
    Aboot Lenin. You've read a guid lot
      In the news – but ken the less o'm?
    Look, Wullie, here is his secret noo
    In a way I can share it wi' you.

baudrons cats   *grun's* grounds

His secret and the secret o' a'
  That's worth ocht.
The shuttles fleein' owre quick for my een
  Prompt the thocht,
And the coordination atween
  Weaver and machine.

The haill shop's dumfounderin'
  To a stranger like me.
Second nature to you; you're perfectly able
  To think, speak and see
Apairt frae the looms, tho' to some
That doesna sae easily come.

Lenin was like that wi' workin' class life,
  At hame wi't a'.
His fause movements couldna been fewer,
  The best weaver Earth ever saw.
A' he'd to dae wi' moved intact,
  Clean, clear, and exact.

A poet like Rilke did the same
  In a different sphere,
Made a single reality – a' a'e 'oo' –
  O' his love and pity and fear;
A seamless garment o' music and thought
But you're owre thrang wi' puirer to tak' tent o't.

What's life or God or what you may ca't
  But something at ane like this?
Can you divide yoursel' frae your breath
  Or – if you say yes –
Frae your mind that as in the case
O' the loom keeps that in its place?

haill whole   puirer poverty
a' a'e 'oo' all one wool   tak' tent o't give your mind to it
thrang preoccupied

59

Empty vessels mak' the maist noise
   As weel you ken.
Still waters rin deep, owre fu' for soond.
   It's the same wi' men.
Belts fleein', wheels birlin' – a river in flood,
Fu' flow and tension o' poo'er and blood.

Are you equal to life as to the loom?
   Turnin' oot shoddy or what?
Claith better than man? D'ye live to the full,
   Your poo'er's a' deliverly taught?
Or scamp a'thing else? Border claith's famous.
Shall things o' mair consequence shame us?

Lenin and Rilke baith gied still mair skill,
   Coopers o' Stobo, to a greater concern
Than you devote to claith in the mill.
   Wad it be ill to learn
To keep a bit eye on their looms as weel
And no' be hailly ta'en up wi' your tweel?

The womenfolk ken what I mean.
   Things maun fit like a glove,
Come clean off the spoon – and syne
   There's time for life and love.
The mair we mak' natural as breathin' the mair
Energy for ither things we'll can spare,
   But as lang as we bide like this
Neist to naething we ha'e, or miss.

Want to gang back to the handloom days?
   Nae fear!
Or paintin' oor hides? Hoo d'ye think we've got
   Frae there to here?

    birlin' spinning   *tweel* cloth
    deliverly consistently   *Neist* next

We'd get a million times faurer still
If maist folk change profits didna leave't till
A wheen here and there to bring it aboot
– Aye, and hindered no' helped to boot.

Are you helpin'? Machinery's improved, but folk?
  Is't no' high time
We were trying' to come into line a' roon?
  (I canna think o' a rhyme).
Machinery in a week mak's greater advances
Than Man's nature twixt Adam and this.

Hundreds to the inch the threids lie in,
  Like the men in a communist cell.
There's a play o' licht frae the factory windas.
  Could you no' mak' mair yoursel'?
Mony a loom mair alive than the weaver seems
For the sun's still nearer than Rilke's dreams.

Ailie Bally's tongue's keepin' time
  To the vibration a' richt.
Clear through the maze your een signal to Jean
  What's for naebody else's sicht.
Short skirts, silk stockin's – fegs, hoo the auld
Emmle-deugs o' the past are curjute and devauld!

And as for me in my fricative work
  I ken fu' weel
Sic an integrity's what I maun ha'e,
  Indivisible, real,
Woven owre close for the point o' a pin
  Onywhere to win in.

wheen few   *curjute* pushed aside
Emmle-deugs rag-ends   *devauld* abandoned

Water of Life

Wha looks on water and's no' affected yet
By memories o' the Flood, and, faurer back,
O' that first flux in which a' life began,
And won sae slowly oot that ony lack
O' poo'er's a shrewd reminder o' the time
   We ploutered in the slime?

It's seldom in my active senses tho'
That water brings sic auld sensations as that
(Gin it's no' mixed wi' something even yet
A wee taet stronger); but in lookin' at
A woman at ony time I mind oor source
   And possible return of course.

Happy wha feels there's solid ground beneath
His feet at ony time – if ony does.
Happy? That's aiblins ga'en a bit owre faur.
I only mean he differs frae me thus
Tho' I'm whiles glad when a less shoogly sea
   Than ithers cradles me.

And if I'm no' aye glad o't it's because
I was sae used to waters as a loon
That I'm amphibious still. A perfect maze
O' waters is about the Muckle Toon,*
Apairt frae't often seemin' through the weather
   That sea and sky swap places a' thegither.

Ah, vivid recollection o' trudgin' that
Crab-like again upon the ocean-flair! –

     *Langholm (the poet's birthplace).

ploutered waded splashing	*shoogly* shaky
taet touch	*-flair* floor
aiblins maybe	

Juist as in lyin' wi' a woman still
I feel a sudden cant and sweesh aince mair
Frae Sodom or Gomorrah wi' yon Eastern whore
    T'oor watery grave o' yore.

She clung to me mair tightly at the end
Than ane expects or wants in sic a case,
Whether frae love or no' I needna say,
A waste o' guid material – her face
Fastened on mine as on a flag a sooker
    And naething shook her.

Although my passion was sair diluted then
I mind the cratur' still frae tip to tae
Better than ony that I've troked wi' syne
– The gowden pendants frae her lugs, her skin
Sae clear that in her cheeks the glints 'ud play
As whiles wi' bits o' looking-glass as loons
    We'd gar the sun loup roon's.

Nae doot the sudden predicament we shared
Has fixed her in my mind abune the lave,
A kind o' compensation for the way
She was sae tashed and lightlied by the wave
Oot o' my recognition and slarried by
    The infernal sly.

A man never faced wi' death kens nocht o' life.
But a' men are? But micht as weel no' be!
The ancient memory is alive to few
And fewer when it is ken what they see,
But them that dae fear neither life nor death,
    Mindin' them baith.

sooker leech	*tashed* soiled
troked wi' had dealings with	*lightlied* slighted
loup dance	*slarried* smeared
abune the lave above the rest	*sly* slime

Nae man can jouk and let the jaw gang by.
To seem to's often to dodge a silly squirt
While bein' whummled in an unseen spate
Lodgin' us securely in faur deeper dirt
Or carryin' us to heichts we canna see
    For th' earth in oor e'e.

Nae gulfs that open 'neath oor feet'll find
Us hailly at a loss if we juist keep
The perspective the deluge should ha' gien's
And if we dinna, or if they're mair deep
Than even that is muckle guidance in,
    It's there altho' we're blin'.

Whatever is to be, what's been has been;
Even if it's hailly undune that deed'll bear
A sense o' sequence forever in itsel',
Implyin', and dependent on, what erst was there,
Tho' it's no' conscious o't – less conscious o't
    Than men o' their historic lot.

Hoo I got oot o' yon I dinna ken,
But I am ready noo at ony time
To be hurled back or forrit to any stage
O' ocht we've ever been twixt sun and slime
Or can become, trustin' what's brocht aboot
    A' th'ither sequels to the water-shute.

Shall wellspring and shower, ebb-tide and neap,
Refuse their separate pairts cryin' let's be ane,
In function as natur', appearance as fact?
Foul here, fair there, to sea and sky again
The river keeps its course and ranges
    Unchanged through a' its changes.

        jouk duck   *whummled* tumbled
        jaw wave

Wha speak o' vice and innocence, peace and war,
Culture and ignorance, humility and pride,
Describe the Fairy Loup, the thunder-plump,
The moss-boil on the moor, the white-topped tide;
And the ane as sune as the tither'll be
   Brocht doon to uniformity.

Ah, weel I ken that ony ane o' them,
Nae maitter hoo vividly I ca't to mind,
Kennin' the world to men's as light to water,
Has endless beauties to which my een are blind,
My ears deaf – aye, and ilka drap a world
   Bigger than a' Mankind has yet unfurled.

from *Work in Progress*

Gin scenic beauty had been a' I sook
I never need ha' left the Muckle Toon.
I saw it there as weel as ony man
(As I'll sune prove); and sin syne I've gane roon'
Hauf o' the warld wi' faculties undulled
      And no' seen't equalled.

But scenic beauty's never maittered much
To me afore, sin poetry isna made
O' onything that's seen, toucht, smelt, or heard,
And no' till lately ha'e the hame scenes played
A pairt in my creative thocht I've yet
      To faddom, and permit.

Gin there's an efter life hoo can I guess
What kind o' man I'll be wha canna tell
What's pairted me here frae my kith and kin

          ca't call it   *sook* sought

In a' airts mair than Heaven is frae Hell
(To bate the question which is which a wee)
    As't seems to them and me,

Nor tell what brings me unexpectedly back
Whaur't seems nae common thocht or interest's left.
Guid kens it wasna snobbery or hate,
Selfishness, ingratitude, or chance that reft
Sae early, sae completely, ties that last
    Maist fowk for life – or was't?

I bein' a man made ither human ties
But they – my choice – are broken (in this case
No' a' my choice) as utterly as those
That bound me to my kin and native place.
My wife and bairns, is't tinin' them that thraws
    Me back on my first cause?

Foreseein' in Christine's or in Walter's mind
A picture o' mysel' as in my ain
My mither rises or I rise in hers
Incredible as to a Martian brain
A cratur' o' this star o' oors micht be
    It had nae point o' contact wi'.

Daith in my faither's case. I ha'e his build,
His energy, but no' his raven hair,
Rude cheeks, clear een. I am whey-faced. My een
Ha'e dark rings roon' them and my pow is fair.
A laddie when he dee'd, I kent little o'm and he
    Kent less o' me.

Gin he had lived my life and wark micht weel
Ha' been entirely different, better or waur,

wee little while	*cratur'* creature
tinin' losing	*pow* head
thraws throws	

66

Or neither, comparison impossible.
It wadna ha' been the same. That's hoo things are.
He had his differences frae some folks aroon'
    But never left the Muckle Toon.

He had his differences but a host o' freen's
At ane wi' him on maist things and at serious odds
In nane, a kindly, gin conscientious, man,
Fearless but peacefu', and to man's and God's
Service gi'en owre accordin' to his lichts
    But fondest o' his ain fireside o' nichts.

Afore he dee'd he turned and gied a lang
Last look at pictures o' my brither and me
Hung on the wa' aside the bed, I've heard
My mither say. I wonder then what he
Foresaw or hoped and hoo – or gin – it squares
    Wi' subsequent affairs.

I've led a vera different life frae ocht
He could conceive or share I ken fu' weel
Yet gin he understood – or understands
(His faith, no' mine) – I like to feel, and feel,
He wadna wish his faitherhood undone
    O' sic an unforeseen unlikely son.

I like to feel, and yet I ken that a'
I mind or think aboot him is nae mair
To what he was, or aiblins is, than yon
Picture o' me at fourteen can compare
Wi' what I look the day (or looked even then).
    He looked in vain, and I again.

Gin he had lived at warst we'd ha' been freen's
Juist as my mither (puir auld soul) and I
– As maist fowk are, no' ga'en vera deep,
A maitter o' easy-ozie habit maistly, shy
O' fundamentals, as it seems to me,
  – A minority o' ane, may be!

Maist bonds 'twixt man and man are weel ca'd bonds.
But I'll come back to this, since come I maun,
Fellow-feelin', common humanity, claptrap (or has
In anither sense my comin'-back begun?)
I've had as little use for, to be terse,
    As maist folk ha'e for verse.

My wife and weans in London never saw
The Muckle Toon that I'm concerned wi' noo
(Sittin' in Liverpool), and never may.
What maitters't then, gin a' life's gantin' through,
Biggit on sicna kittle sands as these,
    Wi' like haphazardries?

My clan is darkness 'yont a wee ring
O' memory showin' catsiller here or there
But nocht complete or lookin' twice the same.
Graham, Murray, Carruthers, Frater, and faur mair
Auld Border breeds than I can tell ha' been
    Woven in its skein.

Great hooses keep their centuried lines complete.
Better than I can mind my faither they
Preserve their forebears painted on their wa's
And can trace ilka tendency and trait
O' bluid and spirit in their divers stages
    Doon the ages.

To mind and body I ha' nae sic clue,
A water flowin' frae an unkent source
Wellin' up in me to catch the licht at last
At this late break in its hidden course,
Yet my blin' instincts nurtured in the dark
    Sing sunwards like the lark.

weans children	*kittle* ticklish
gantin' gaping	*catsiller* mica
Biggit built	

I canna signal to a single soul
In a' the centuries that led up to me
In happy correspondence, yet to a'
These nameless thanks for strength and cleanness gi'e,
And mair, auld Border breeds, ken I inherit,
    And croun, your frontier spirit.

Reivers to weavers and to me. Weird way!
Yet in the last analysis I've sprung
Frae battles, mair than ballads, and it seems
The thrawn auld water has at last upswung
Through me, and's mountin' like the vera devil
    To its richt level!

(from The Modern Scot, July 1931)

By Wauchopeside

Thrawn water? Aye, owre thrawn to be aye thrawn!
I ha'e my wagtails like the Wauchope tae,
Birds fu' o' fechtin' spirit, and o' fun,
That whiles jig in the air in lichtsome play
Like glass-ba's on a fountain, syne stand still
Save for a quiver, shoot up an inch or twa, fa' back
Like a swarm o' winter-gnats, or are tost aside,
      By their inclination's kittle loup,
      To balance efter hauf a coup.

There's mair in birds than men ha'e faddomed yet.
Tho' maist churn oot the stock sangs o' their kind
There's aiblins genius here and there; and aince
'Mang whitebeams, hollies, siller birks –

reivers freebooters	*loup* jump
thrawn stubborn	*coup* tumble
Thrawn cross-grained	*aiblins* maybe
kittle unpredictable	*siller birks* silver birches

The tree o' licht –
I mind
I used to hear a blackie mony a nicht
Singin' awa' t'an unconscionable 'oor
Wi' nocht but the water keepin't company
(Or nocht that ony human ear could hear)
– And wondered if the blackie heard it either
Or cared whether it was singin' tae or no'!
O there's nae sayin' what my verses awn
To memories like these. Ha'e I come back
To find oot? Or to borrow mair? Or see
Their helpless puirness to what gar'd them be?
Late sang the blackie but it stopt at last.
The river still ga'ed singin' past.

O there's nae sayin' what my verses awn
To memories, or my memories to me.
But a'e thing's certain; ev'n as things stand
I could vary them in coontless ways and gi'e
Wauchope a new course in the minds o' men,
The blackie gowden feathers, and the like,
And yet no' cease to be dependent on
The things o' Nature, and create insteid
Oot o' my ain heid
Or get ootside the range
O' trivial change
Into that cataclysmic country which
Natheless a' men inhabit – and enrich.

For civilization in its struggle up
Has mair than seasonal changes o' ideas,
Glidin' through periods o' flooers and fruit,
Winter and Spring again; to cope wi' these
Is difficult eneuch to tax the patience
O' Methuselah himsel' – but transformations,

awn owe

Yont physical and mental habits, symbols, rites,
That mak' sic changes nane, are aye gaen on,
Revolutions in the dynasty o' live ideals
–The stuff wi' which alane true poetry deals.
Wagtail or water winna help me here,
(That's clearer than Wauchope at its clearest's clear!)
Where the life o' a million years is seen
Like a louch look in a lass's een.

(from The Modern Scot, April 1932)

Whuchulls*

Il ne peut y avoir du progrès (vrai, c'est-à-dire moral), que dans l'individu et par l'individu lui-même.   CHARLES BAUDELAIRE

Gie owre your coontin', for nae man can tell
The population o' a wud like this
In plants and beasts, and needna pride himsel'
On ocht he marks by a' he's boond to miss.
What is oor life that we should prize't abune
Lichen's or slug's o' which we ken scarce mair
Than they o' oors when a' thing's said and dune,
Or fancy it ser's "heicher purposes"?
The wice man kens that a fool's brain and his
Differ at maist as little 'gainst a' that is
As different continents and centuries,
Time, station, caste, culture, or character –
Triflin' distinctions that dinna cairry faur –
And if at ony point he stops and says:
"My lot has fa'n in mair enlightened days,
I'm glad to be a European, no' a black
– Human, no' hotchin' glaur," ahint his back
Let him forehear as foolish a future set

*Local pronunciation of Whitshiels, a wood near Langholm.

louch clouded	*hotchin'* seething
Gie owre leave off	*glaur* slime
heicher higher	

Him in a class as seemin' laicher yet,
Or ten pasts damn him for a graceless get.
Original forest, Whuchulls, public park,
Mysel', or ony man, beast, mineral, weed,
I clearly see are a' aside the mark.
The poet hauds nae brief for ony kind,
Age, place, or range o' sense, and no' confined
To ony nature can share Creation's insteed.
First speir this bowzie bourach if't prefers
The simmer or the winter, day or night,
New or forhooied nests, rain's pelts or smirrs,
Bare sticks or gorded fullyery; and syne invite
My choice twixt good and evil, life and death.
What hoar trunk girds at ivy or at fug
Or what sleek bole complains it lacks them baith?
Nae foliage hustle-farrant in windy light
Is to the Muse a mair inspirin' sight
Than fungus poxy as the mune; nae blight
A meaner state than flourish at its height.
Leafs' music weel accords wi' gloghole's glug.
Then cite nae mair this, that, or onything.
To nae belief or preference I cling,
Earth – let alane the mucklest mountain in't –
Is faur owre kittle a thing to hide ahint.
I'll no' toy wi' the fragments o't I ken
– Nor seek to beshield *it*, least o' a' men! . . .
Yet here's a poem takin' shape again,
Inevitable shape, faur mair inevitable
Than birks and no' bamboos or banyans here,
Impredictable, relentless, thriddin' the rabble

laicher lower	*fullyery* foliage
speir ask	*fug* moss
bowzie branchy	*hustle-farrant* tattered
bourach cluster	*gloghole* deep hole
forhooied forsaken	*mucklest* highest
smirrs drizzles	*kittle* ticklish
gorded fullblown	*thriddin'* threading

O' themes and aspects in this thrawart scene.
O freedom constrainin' me as nae man's been
Mair constrained wha wasna, as I'll yet be, freer! ...

"Clearlier it comes. I winna ha'e it. Quick
And gi'e me tutors in arboriculture then.
Let me plunge where the undergrowth's mair thick.
Experts in forestry, botany — a' that ken
Mair than I dae o' onything that's here.
I ken sae little it easily works its will.
Fence me frae its design wi' endless lear.
Pile up the facts and let me faurer ben.
Multiply my vocabulary ten times ten.
Let me range owre a' prosody again.
Mak' yon a lammergeir, no' juist a wren.
Is that owre muckle for a Scotsman yet,
Needin' a soupler leid, great skills, he lacks?
Is he in silence safer frae attacks?
Yet wha can thole to see it cavalierly choose
In God's green wud — tak' this and that refuse?
Yon knoul-taed trees, this knurl, at least 't'll use!
Gar memory gie the place fower seasons at aince."
The world's no' mine. I'll tak' nae hen's care o't.
"Is that Creation's nature you evince,
Sma-bookin' Whuchulls to a rice or twa
Sae arbitrarily picked, and voidin' a'
The lave as gin it wasna worth a jot?"

There is nae reason but on unreason's based
And needs to mind that often to hain its sense,

thrawart perverse	*thole* bear
lear learning	*knoul-taed* swollen-toed
faurer ben further in	*fower* four
yon that	*Sma-bookin'* shrinking
muckle much	*rice* branch
soupler suppler	*lave* rest
leid language	*hain* keep

Dodo and Mammoth had the same misplaced
Trust in their *données* – and hae lang gane hence.
Why fash sae muckle owre Nature's present stock
In view o' a' past changes and to come?
It's wipin' oot 'ud be nae greater shock
Than mony afore; and Poetry isna some
Society for Preservin' Threatened Types,
But strokes a cat or fiddles on its tripes,
And for inclusions or exclusions, fegs,
Needna apologize while a'e bird's eggs
Are plain, anither's speckled, beasts ha'e legs,
Birds wings, Earth here brairds trees, here nocht but seggs.
'Troth it's an insult for a man to seek
A'e woman owre anither. A' women hae
Their differences and resemblances, but whatna freak
Thinks, frae the latter, ony ane'll dae
Or, frae the former, fain 'ud sair them a'?

The world o' a' the senses is the same.
Creation disna live frae hand to mooth
Juist improvisin' as it gangs, forsooth,
And there's nae meanin' in life that bode to da'
Until we came – or bides a wicer day –
'Yont brute creation, fools, bairns, unborn, deid.
I'd sing bird-mooth'd wi' ony ither creed,
No' wi' Creation's nature and its aim;
Or sing like Miffy – wheesht, world, while he speaks.
In English – hence, the Universal Speech.
He has nae wings; let birds pit on the breeks.
Nae fins. Fish, copy him! And sae let each
O' Nature's sorts be modelled upon him
Frae animalculae to Seraphim.

fash bother	*fain 'ud sair* gladly would serve
muckle much	*bode to da'* waited to dawn
brairds sprouts	*wicer* wiser
seggs marsh plants	*breeks* trousers

He is nae poet, but likes the Laureate best.
What, write like that? – Ah! here's the crucial test!
I ha'e the courage to be a Scotsman then
(Nae Scot'll e'er be Laureate we ken!)*
Divided frae ither folk to Eternity's en',
And, if I hadna, ken it wadna maitter.
I'd be it still. Exclusive forms are nature.
It means to be and comes in Nature's way.
– In its ain nature's, as a' in Nature does.
Supersessions, innovations, variations, display
Nature, no' hide; and Scotland, Whuchulls, us
Interest me less for what they are than as
Facts o' the creative poo'er that, tho' they pass,
'll aye be qualified by their ha'en been.
It is nae treason then to stell my een
No' on their fleetin' shapes but on their deep
Constituent principles destined to keep
A mystery greater than the sight o' eels
Kelterin' through a' the seven seas reveals.
These to a'e spot converge, but we gang oot
Aye faurer frae oor source – ne'er back, I doot.
"I like to see the ramel gowd-bestreik,
And sclaffer cuit-deep through the birsled leafs.
Here I dung doon the squirrels wi' my sling
And made the lassies brooches o' their paws,
Set girns for rabbits and for arnuts socht,
Herried my nests and blew the eggs, and lit
Fires o' fir-burrs and hag in tinker style.
Hoo faur the interests o' progress warrant
Meddlin' wi' Whuchulls' auld amenities,

*"There are poets little enough to envy even a poet-laureate." – *Gray*

stell fix	*dung* knocked
Kelterin' snaking	*girns* snares
ramel branches	*arnuts* earth-nuts
gowd-bestreik gold-veined	*Herried* plundered
sclaffer shuffle	*-burrs* -cones
cuit-deep ankle deep	*hag* peat
birsled crackled	

And their dependent livelihoods and ploys,
I'm no' to say; I'm glad to see it still
Temporarily triumphant against control.
It's pleasant nae doot for a woman to dream
O' yieldin' hersel' to some buirdly man
Wha kens what he wants and willy-nilly'll ha'e't
But when the time comes she'll aye find, I think,
Guid reasons for no' yieldin' – bless her hert!
Sae wi' the Whuchulls. May the Lord be praised."
Nae doot primeval beasts felt juist the same
Aboot the place – tho' different frae this
As ony change that's still in store for it.
Hauf saurian-emeritus, hauf prentice spook,
You'll never see the plantin' for the trees,
This Eden where Adam comes fu' circle yet.

There is nae ither way. For weel or woe
It is attained. Tho' idle side-winds blow
In on me still and inferior questions thraw
Their crockets up, a' doots and torments cease.
The road is clear. I gang in perfect peace,
And my idea spreids and shines and lures me on,
O lyric licht auld chaos canna dam!
Celestial, soothin', sanctifyin' course, wi' a'
The high sane forces o' the sacred time
Fechtin' on my side through it till I con
This blainy blanderin' and ken that I'm
Delivered frae the need o' trauchlin' wi't,
Accommodated to't, but in my benmaist hert
Acknowledgementless, free, condition or reform,
Or sunny lown or devastatin' storm,
Indifferent to me; where the Arts stert
Wi' a' else *corpore vili* – "God's mercy-seat!"

(from *The Modern Scot*, January 1933)

buirdly well-built
plantin' plantation
blainy blanderin' patchy sowing

trauchlin' struggling
benmaist inmost
lown calm

from

SCOTS UNBOUND AND OTHER POEMS

(1932)

The Back o' Beyond

Bend doon, the sunsmite oot o' your een,
To this lanely pool and see
A'e shadow gantin' 'mang shadows there
And mind aince mair wi' me
Hoo months afore they were born
Mony a fine simmer's day
'S come doon through their mither's joy
To where men lay.

Stand up; and at midday yet
What a glunsh we get!

Milk-wort and Bog-cotton

To Seumas O'Sullivan

Cwa' een like milk-wort and bog-cotton hair!
I love you, earth, in this mood best o' a'
When the shy spirit like a laich wind moves
And frae the lift nae shadow can fa'
Since there's nocht left to thraw a shadow there
Owre een like milk-wort and milk-white cotton hair.

Wad that nae leaf upon anither wheeled
A shadow either and nae root need dern
In sacrifice to let sic beauty be!

gantin' yawning	*lift* sky
glunsh dull look	*Wad* would
Cwa' come	*dern* hide
laich light	

77

But deep surroondin' darkness I discern
Is aye the price o' licht. Wad licht revealed
Naething but you, and nicht nocht else concealed.

Lynch-pin
To "Æ"

Here where I sit assembling in the sun
The salient features o' my structure o' banes
I feel that somewhere there's a missing one
That mak's a dish o' whummle o' my pains.
Sma' but the clue to a' the rest, and no'
In ony woman hidden nor on this earth,
And if there's ony ither world, hoo it's got there,
If't has, I ken nae mair than hoo I ken my dearth
That yet fills my haill life wi' the effort
To embody a' creation – and find this ort.

Why I Became a Scots Nationalist

Gi'e me Scots-room in life and love
And set me then my smeddum to prove
In scenes like these. Like Pushkin I,
My time for flichty conquests by,
Valuing nae mair some quick-fire cratur'
Wha hurries up the ways o' natur',
Am happy, when after lang and sair
Pursuit you yield yoursel' to me,
But wi' nae rapture, cauldly there,
Open but glowerin' callously,
Yet slow but surely heat until
You catch my flame against your will
And the mureburn tak's the hill.

whummle nothing	*smeddum* mettle
haill whole	*mureburn* moor-burning
ort scrap	

Dytiscus

The problem in the pool is plain.
Must men to higher things ascend
For air like the Dytiscus there,
Breathe through their spiracles, and turn
To diving bells and seek their share
Of sustenance in the slime again
Till they clear life, as he his pool
To starve in purity, the fool,
Their finished faculties mirrored, fegs,
Foiled-fierce as his three pairs of legs?
Praise be Dytiscus-men are rare.
Life's pool still foul and full of fare.
Long till to suicidal success attain
We water-beetles of the brain!

from *The Oon Olympian*

Consciousness springs frae unplumbed deeps
And maist o' men mak' haste
To kep odd draps in shallow thoughts
    And let the rest rin waste.
Quickly forgettin' ocht they catch
    Depends upon the kittle coorse
O' a wilder fount than they daur watch
Free-springin' in its native force
Against the darkness o' its source.

Wha fear the cataract and like
    Some spigot's drip instead,
Wha prate o' laws and turn blin' een,

Oon empty   *kittle* wayward
kep catch

79

On the anarchy that's gied,
    Owreshadowed wi' its chaos still,
Even sic puir arbitrary forms
May weel haud to – they need them ill –
Thoughts faur frae elementary storms
Tricklin' through thin domestic pipes
To their wee ta'en-forgrantit types.

Auld Goethe never wet his feet
    But had the water laid on
Baith H. and C., nor kent nor cared
    The deeps his pipes made raid on,
A michty expert on H_2O
Almaist hailly in terms o' taps
Plus a shoo'er o' rain, a river's flow,
Even a keek at the sea perhaps
– But Oh! that the Heavens had opened and let
A second Flood on this plumbers' pet!

Hoist them like ba's, ye fountains, yet
    Upon your loupin' jets,
O' wha's irregular ups and doons
Nae metronome the measure gets,
The fools wha think that they can pose
    As authorities on thought
Yet daurna look whence it arose
Nor faddom the conditionin' o't
– And let the bobbin' craturs think
It's them that gars you rise and sink!

Of John Davidson

I remember one death in my boyhood
That next to my father's, and darker, endures;

loupin' jumping

Not Queen Victoria's, but Davidson, yours,
And something in me has always stood
Since then looking down the sandslope
On your small black shape by the edge of the sea,
– A bullet-hole through a great scene's beauty,
God through the wrong end of a telescope.

from

STONY LIMITS AND OTHER POEMS
(1934)

The Skeleton of the Future
(At Lenin's Tomb)

Red granite and black diorite, with the blue
Of the labradorite crystals gleaming like precious
       stones
In the light reflected from the snow; and behind them
The eternal lightning of Lenin's bones.

In the Foggy Twilight

I lay in the foggy twilight
In a hollow o' the hills and saw
Moisture getherin' slowly on the heather cowes
In drops no' quite heavy eneuch to fa'.

And I kent I was still like that
Wi' the spirit o' God, alas!;
Lyin' in wait in vain for a single grey drop
To quicken into perfect quidditas.

cowes bushes

81

First Love

I have been in this garden of unripe fruit
  All the long day,
Where cold and clear from the hard green apples
  The light fell away.

I was wandering here with my own true love,
  But as I bent o'er,
She dwindled back to her childhood again
  And I saw her no more.

A wind sprang up and a hail of buds
  About me rolled,
Then this fog I knew before I was born
  But now – cold, cold!

from *Shetland Lyrics*
With the Herring Fishers

"I see herrin'." – I hear the glad cry
And 'gainst the moon see ilka blue jowl
In turn as the fishermen haul on the nets
And sing: "Come, shove in your heids and growl."

"Soom on, bonnie herrin', soom on," they shout,
Or "Come in, O come in, and see me."
"Come gie the auld man something to dae.
It'll be a braw change frae the sea."

O it's ane o' the bonniest sichts in the warld
To watch the herrin' come walkin' on board
In the wee sma' 'oors o' a simmer's mornin'
As if o' their ain accord.

Soom swim   *wee sma' 'oors* earliest hours
braw fine

For this is the way that God sees life,
The haill jing-bang o's appearin'
Up owre frae the edge o' naethingness
– It's his happy cries I'm hearin'.

"Left, right – O come in and see me,"
Reid and yellow and black and white
Toddlin' up into Heaven thegither
At peep o' day frae the endless night.

"I see herrin'," I hear his glad cry,
And 'gainst the moon see his muckle blue jowl,
As he handles buoy-tow and bush-raip
Singin': "Come, shove in your heids and growl!"

from *The War with England*

The social scene could be little
   But confusion and loss to me,
And, Scotland, better than all your towns
   Was a bed of moss to me.
I had to lie on the hills and watch
The founts that to keep their tryst
Had found their way through the wards of the rock
Slower than the second coming of Christ
   To know how my task was priced.

I was better with the sounds of the sea
   Than with the voices of men
And in desolate and desert places
   I found myself again.
For the whole of the world came from these
And he who returns to the source
May gauge the worth of the outcome
And approve and perhaps reinforce
Or disapprove and perhaps change its course.

haill whole   *bush-raip* drift-net rope

Now I deal with the hills at their roots
    And the streams at their springs
And am to the land that I love
    As he who brings
His bride home, and they know each other
Not as erst, like their friends, they have done,
But carnally, casually, knowing that only
By life nigh undone can life be begun,
    And accept and are one.
    When was anything born in Scotland last,
    Risks taken and triumphs won?

Cattle Show

I shall go among red faces and virile voices,
See stylish sheep, with fine heads and well-wooled,
And great bulls mellow to the touch,
Brood mares of marvellous approach, and geldings
With sharp and flinty bones and silken hair.

And through th'enclosure draped in red and gold
I shall pass on to spheres more vivid yet
Where countesses' coque feathers gleam and glow
And, swathed in silks, the painted ladies are
Whose laughter plays like summer lightning there.

John MacLean (*1879–1923*)

All the buildings in Glasgow are grey
With cruelty and meanness of spirit,
But once in a while one greyer than the rest
    A song shall merit
Since a miracle of true courage is seen
For a moment its walls between.

Look at it, you fools, with unseeing eyes
And deny it with lying lips!
But your craven bowels well know what it is
          And hasten to eclipse
In a cell, as black as the shut boards of the Book
You lie by, the light no coward can brook.

It is not the blue of heaven that colours
The blue jowls of your thugs of police,
And "justice" may well do its filthy work
          Behind walls as filthy as these
And congratulate itself blindly and never know
The prisoner takes the light with him as he goes
     below.

Stand close, stand close, and block out the light
As long as you can, you ministers and lawyers,
Hulking brutes of police, fat bourgeoisie,
Sleek derma for congested guts – its fires
Will leap through yet; already it is clear
Of all MacLean's foes not one was his peer.

As Pilate and the Roman soldiers to Christ
Were Law and Order to the finest Scot of his day,
One of the few true men in our sordid breed,
A flash of sun in a country all prison-grey.
Speak to others of Christian charity; I cry again
For vengeance on the murderers of John MacLean.

Let the light of truth in on the base pretence
Of Justice that sentenced him behind these grey walls.
All law is the contemptible fraud he declared it.
Like a lightning-bolt at last the workers' wrath falls
On all such castles of cowards whether they be
Uniformed in ermine, or blue, or khaki.

Royal honours for murderers and fools! The "fount
     of honour"

Is poisoned and spreads its corruption all through,
But Scotland will think yet of the broken body
And unbreakable spirit, MacLean, of you,
And know you were indeed the true tower of its
    strength,
As your prison of its foul stupidity, at length.

from *Ode to All Rebels*

*In his appearance not overdazzling; so that you
might without difficulty recognize him as belonging
to that class of men of letters who are continuously
hated by the Rich.* PETRONIUS, *Satiricon* lxxxiii.

*Wherefore are all they happy that deal very
treacherously?* Jeremiah xii, 1 (Vulgate).

I mind when my first wife died.
    I was a young fella then,
Strang, and ta'en up wi' life, and she'd come
    By a sudden and terrible en',
My haill warld gane – but I was livin' on
    Tho' hoo I could hardly ken.
Yet even in the middle o' kistin' her
In the hour o' my grief I felt the stir
    O' auld feelin's again.
Feelin's I had when I courted her first,
No' syne, and hated noo and cursed.
Hoo could I trust love again if a'
The tender ties twixt us twa
Like this could be wantonly snapt,
While afore her corpse was decently hapt
I was kindlin' aince mair in a different airt,
My rude bluid warnin' my woe for its pairt
It 'bood ha'e anither wife, and sune?

kistin' coffining	*airt* place
hapt buried	*'bood* had to

86

Nay, I felt the cratur juist hoverin' roon.
At ony meenut her face 'ud kyth.
– Ahint my dule and self-scunner already,
    My Second, you were skinklan' blithe.
'Or I kent gin you'd be virgin or widdy,
    A thocht I mind ha'en
Even as frae lowerin' the coffin I raze
Conscious o' my nature in a wud amaze
And strauchtened up my muckle animal frame
That kent what it wanted and kent nae shame
    And stood in a burst o' sun
    Glowerin' at the bit broken grun'.

                    *

    I ha'ena seen the bairns
    Since Jean divorced me
– Mona and Fergus and wee Peter –
    And never mair may see,
    – Save whiles in memory.
Yet I lo'ed them as dearly as ony man
    Can lo'e his spawn
– Tho' I hated to see repetitions
    In them o' her and me,
Juist "cauld kail het again"
As in maist ither folk I see,
Till as wi' second mairrage that tae
Wi' my taste began to agree,
That, and even the measure they had
    O' common humanity,
They're developin' differently nae doot
    Than if I'd still been aboot
But whether for better or waur
    Or neither wha can say?

kyth appear	*grun'* ground
dule sorrow	*cauld kail het again* cold cabbage
skinklan' sparkling	heated up
widdy widow	*waur* worse
wud mad	

I'd hae hated like Hell I ken
　　To influence them ony way.
Yet my absence may ha'e dune that tae.
　　I wadna ken the bairns
　　Even if I saw them again.
What I mind o' them canna correspond
　　Wi' what they've grown, that's plain,
And the faitherly instinct isna sae deep
　　As to tell me they're my ain.
We need propinquity and habit then
　　Oor bairns to ken
And reason and feelin' are o' nae avail
　　When these handrails fail,
And it's only for a wee while we can recognise
　　– If ever – what nearest to us lies.

Harry Semen

I ken these islands each inhabited
Forever by a single man
Livin' in his separate world as only
In dreams yet maist folk can.

Mine's like the moonwhite belly o' a hoo
Seen in the water as a fisher draws in his line.
I canna land it nor can it ever brak awa'.
It never moves, yet seems a' movement in the brine;
A movin' picture o' the spasm frae which I was born,
It writhes again, and back to it I'm willy-nilly torn.
A' men are similarly fixt; and the difference 'twixt
　　The sae-ca'd sane and insane
Is that the latter whiles ha'e glimpses o't
　　And the former nane.

Particle frae particle'll brak asunder,
Ilk ane o' them mair livid than the neist.
A separate life? – incredible war o' equal lichts,
　　　　hoo dogfish

88

Nane o' them wi' ocht in common in the least.
Nae threid o' a' the fabric o' my thocht
Is left alangside anither; a pack
O' leprous scuts o' weasels riddlin' a plaid
    Sic thrums could never mak'.
Hoo mony shades o' white gaed curvin' owre
To yon blae centre o' her belly's flower?
Milk-white, and dove-grey, wi' harebell veins.
Ae scar in fair hair like the sun in sunlicht lay,
And pelvic experience in a thin shadow line;
Thocht canna mairry thocht as sic saft shadows dae.

Grey ghastly commentaries on my puir life,
A' the sperm that's gane for naething rises up to damn
In sick-white onanism the single seed
Frae which in sheer irrelevance I cam.
What were the odds against me? Let me coont.
What worth am I to a' that micht ha'e been?
To a' the wasted slime I'm capable o'
Appeals this lurid emission, whirlin' lint-white and
    green.
Am I alane richt, solidified to life,
Disjoined frae a' this searin' like a white-het knife,
And vauntin' my alien accretions here,
Boastin' sanctions, purpose, sense the endless tide
I cam frae lacks – the tide I still sae often feed?
O bitter glitter; wet sheet and flowin' sea – and what
    beside?

Sae the bealin' continents lie upon the seas,
    Sprawlin' in shapeless shapes a' airts,
Like ony splash that ony man can mak'
    Frae his nose or throat or ither pairts,
Fantastic as ink through blottin'-paper rins.
But this is white, white like a flooerin' gean,

    thrums threads   *a' airts* all directions
    blae blue   *gean* wild cherry
    bealin' festering

Passin' frae white to purer shades o' white,
Ivory, crystal, diamond, till nae difference is seen
Between its fairest blossoms and the stars
Or the clear sun they melt into,
And the wind mixes them amang each ither
Forever, hue upon still mair dazzlin' hue.

Sae Joseph may ha'e pondered; sae a snawstorm
Comes whirlin' in grey sheets frae the shadowy sky
And only in a sma' circle are the separate flakes seen.
White, whiter, they cross and recross as capricious
     they fly,
Mak' patterns on the grund and weave into wreaths,
Load the bare boughs, and find lodgements in corners
     frae
The scourin' wind that sends a snawstorm up frae the
     earth
To meet that frae the sky, till which is which nae man
     can say.
They melt in the waters. They fill the valleys. They
     scale the peaks.
There's a tinkle o' icicles. The topmaist summit shines
     oot.
Sae Joseph may ha'e pondered on the coiled fire in
     his seed,
The transformation in Mary, and seen Jesus tak' root.

Skald's Death

I have known all the storms that roll.
I have been a singer after the fashion
Of my people – a poet of passion.
     All that is past.
Quiet has come into my soul.
Life's tempest is done.
     I lie at last
A bird cliff under the midnight sun.

from

SECOND HYMN TO LENIN

(1935)

Second Hymn to Lenin

To my friends Naomi Mitchison and Henry Carr

Ah, Lenin, you were richt. But I'm a poet
(And you c'ud mak allowances for that!)
Aimin' at mair than you aimed at
Tho' yours comes first, I know it.

An unexamined life is no' worth ha'in'.
Yet Burke was richt; owre muckle concern
Wi' Life's foundations is a sure
Sign o' decay; tho' Joyce in turn

Is richt, and the principal question
Aboot a work o' art is frae hoo deep
A life it springs – and syne hoo faur
Up frae't it has the poo'er to leap.

And hoo muckle it lifts up wi' it
Into the sunlicht like a saumon there,
Universal Spring! for Morand's richt –
It s'ud be like licht in the air –

> *Are my poems spoken in the factories and fields,*
>   *In the streets o' the toon?*
> *Gin they're no', then I'm failin' to dae*
>   *What I ocht to ha' dune.*

> *Gin I canna win through to the man in the street,*
>   *The wife by the hearth,*
> *A' the cleverness on earth'll no' mak' up*
>   *For the damnable dearth.*

> *"Haud on, haud on; what poet's dune that?*
> *Is Shakespeare read,*
> *Or Dante or Milton or Goethe or Burns?"*
> *— You heard what I said.*

– A means o' world locomotion,
The maist perfected and aerial o' a'.
Lenin's name's gane owre the haill earth,
But the names o' the ithers? – Ha!

What hidie-hole o' the vineyard d' they scart
Wi' minds like the look on a hen's face,
Morand, Joyce, Burke and the rest
That e'er wrote; me noo in like case?

Great poets hardly onybody kens o'?
Geniuses like a man talkin' t'msel'?
Nonsense! They're nocht o' the sort.
Their character's easy to tell.

They're nocht but romantic rebels
Strikin' dilettante poses;
Trotsky – Christ, no' wi' a croon o' thorns
But a wreath o' paper roses.

A' that's great is free and expansive.
What ha' they expanded tae?
They've affected nocht but a fringe
O' mankind in ony way.

Barbarian saviour o' civilisation
Hoo weel ye kent (we're owre dullwitted)
Naething is dune save as we ha'e
Means to en's transparently fitted.

haill whole   *scart* scratch at

Poetry like politics maun cut
The cackle and pursue real ends,
Unerringly as Lenin, and to that
Its nature better tends.

Wi' Lenin's vision equal poet's gift
And what unparallelled force was there!
Nocht in a' literature wi' that
Begins to compare.

Nae simple rhymes for silly folk
But the haill art, as Lenin gied
Nae Marx-withoot-tears to workin' men
But the fu' course instead.

Organic constructional work,
Practicality, and work by degrees;
First things first; and poetry in turn
'Ll be built by these.

You saw it faur off when you thocht
O' mass-education yet.
Hoo lang till they rise to Pushkin?
And that's but a fit!

Oh, it's nonsense, nonsense, nonsense,
Nonsense at this time o' day
That breid-and-butter problems
S'ud be in ony man's way.

They s'ud be like the tails we tint
On leavin' the monkey stage;
A' maist folk fash aboot's alike
Primaeval to oor age.

fit step   *fash* care
tint shed

93

We're grown-up folk that haena yet
Put bairnly things aside
– A' that's material and moral –
And oor new state descried.

Sport, love, and parentage,
Trade, politics, and law
S'ud be nae mair to us than braith
We hardly ken we draw.

Freein' oor poo'ers for greater things,
And fegs there's plenty o' them,
Tho' wha's still trammelt in alow
Canna be tenty o' them –

In the meantime Montéhus' sangs –
But as you were ready to tine
The Russian Revolution to the **German**
Gin that ser'd better syne,

Or foresaw that Russia maun lead
The workers' cause, and then
Pass the lead elsewhere, and aiblins
Fa' faur backward again,

Sae here, twixt poetry and politics,
There's nae doot in the en'.
Poetry includes that and s'ud be
The greatest poo'er amang men.

– It's the greatest, *in posse* at least,
That men ha'e discovered yet
Tho' nae doot they're unconscious still
O' ithers faur greater than it.

bairnly childish	*ser'd* served
alow deep down	*aiblins* perhaps
tenty mindful	*poo'er* power
tine give up	

You confined yoursel' to your work
– A step at a time;
But, as the loon is in the man,
That'll be ta'en up i' the rhyme,

Ta'en up like a pool in the sands
Aince the tide rows in,
When life opens its hert and sings
Withoot scruple or sin.

Your knowledge in your ain sphere
Was exact and complete
But your sphere's elementary and sune by
As a poet maun see't.

For a poet maun see in a'thing,
Ev'n what looks trumpery or horrid,
A subject equal to ony
– A star for the forehead!

A poet has nae choice left
Betwixt Beaverbrook, say, and God,
Jimmy Thomas or you,
A cat, carnation, or clod.

He daurna turn awa' frae ocht
For a single act o' neglect
And straucht he may fa' frae grace
And be void o' effect.

Disinterestedness,
Oor profoundest word yet,
But hoo faur yont even that
The sense o' onything's set!

loon boy   daurna dare not
rows rolls   straucht at once
sune by soon done with

The inward necessity yont
Ony laws o' cause
The intellect conceives
That a'thing has!

Freend, foe; past, present, future;
Success, failure; joy, fear;
Life, Death; and a'thing else,
For us, are equal here.

Male, female; quick or deid,
Let us fike nae mair;
The deep line o' cleavage
Disna lie there.

Black in the pit the miner is,
The shepherd reid on the hill,
And I'm wi' them baith until
The end of mankind, I wis.

Whatever their jobs a' men are ane
In life, and syne in daith
(Tho' it's sma' patience I can ha'e
Wi' life's ideas o' that by the way)
And he's nae poet but kens it, faith,
And ony job but the hardest's ta'en.

The sailor gangs owre the curve o' the sea,
The hoosewife's thrang in the wash-tub,
And whatna rhyme can I find but hub,
And what else can poetry be?

The core o' a' activity,
Changin't in accordance wi'
Its inward necessity
And mede o' integrity.

fike vex (ourselves)   *mede* measure
thrang busy

Unremittin', relentless,
Organized to the last degree,
Ah, Lenin, politics is bairns' play
To what this maun be!

On the Ocean Floor

Now more and more on my concern with the lifted waves
            of genius gaining
I am aware of the lightless depths that beneath them lie;
And as one who hears their tiny shells incessantly raining
On the ocean floor as the foraminifera die.

With a Lifting of the Head

ὑπεροχῇ της ἐαυτῶν κεφαλῆς — PLOTINUS

Scotland, when it is given to me
            As it will be
To sing the immortal song
The crown of all my long
            Travail with thee
I know in that high hour
I'll have, and use, the power
Sublime contempt to blend
With its ecstatic end,
As who, in love's embrace,
Forgetfully may frame
Above the poor slut's face
Another woman's name.

At the Cenotaph

Are the living so much use
That we need to mourn the dead?
Or would it yield better results

bairns' children's

To reverse their roles instead?
The millions slain in the War –
Untimely, the best of our seed? –
Would the world be any the better
If they were still living indeed?
The achievements of such as are
To the notion lend no support;
The whole history of life and death
Yields no scrap of evidence for't. –
Keep going to your wars, you fools, as of yore;
I'm the civilisation you're fighting for.

At the Graveside

There is no stupid soul who neither knows
The rudiments of human history
Nor seeks to solve the problems of this life
But still must give his witless testimony
On huge conundrums. – Faithless in small things,
Let all such cease their fond imaginings.
The eyes of fools are on the ends of God.
I postpone all such thoughts beneath this sod.

Light and Shadow

Like memories of what cannot be
Within the reign of memory . . .
That shake our mortal frames to dust.   SHELLEY

On every thought I have the countless shadows fall
Of other thoughts as valid that I cannot have;
Cross-lights of errors, too, impossible to me,
Yet somehow truer than all these thoughts, being with more
power aglow.

May I never lose these shadowy glimpses of unknown thoughts
That modify and minify my own, and never fail
To keep some shining sense of the way all thoughts at last
Before life's dawning meaning like the stars at sunrise pale.

In the Children's Hospital

Does it matter? Losing your legs?   SIEGFRIED SASSOON

Now let the legless boy show the great lady
How well he can manage his crutches.
It doesn't matter though the Sister objects,
"He's not used to them yet," when such is
The will of the Princess. Come, Tommy,
Try a few desperate steps through the ward.
Then the hand of Royalty will pat your head
And life suddenly cease to be hard.
For a couple of legs are surely no miss
When the loss leads to such an honour as this!
One knows, when one sees how jealous the rest
Of the children are, it's been all for the best! –
But would the sound of your sticks on the floor
Thundered in her skull for evermore!

Lo! a Child is Born

I thought of a house where the stones seemed suddenly changed
And became instinct with hope, hope as solid as themselves,
And the atmosphere warm with that lovely heat,
The warmth of tenderness and longing souls, the smiling anxiety
That rules a home where a child is about to be born.
The walls were full of ears. All voices were lowered.
Only the mother had the right to groan or complain.
Then I thought of the whole world. Who cares for its travail
And seeks to encompass it in like lovingkindness and peace?
There is a monstrous din of the sterile who contribute nothing
To the great end in view, and the future fumbles,
A bad birth, not like the child in that gracious home
Heard in the quietness turning in its mother's womb,
A strategic mind already, seeking the best way
To present himself to life, and at last, resolved,
Springing into history quivering like a fish,

Dropping into the world like a ripe fruit in due time. –
But where is the Past to which Time, smiling through her tears
At her new-born son, can turn crying: "I love you"?

Another Epitaph on an Army
of Mercenaries*

It is a God-damned lie to say that these
Saved, or knew, anything worth any man's pride.
They were professional murderers and they took
Their blood money and impious risks and died.
In spite of all their kind some elements of worth
With difficulty persist here and there on earth.

The Two Parents

I love my little son, and yet when he was ill
I could not confine myself to his bedside.
I was impatient of his squalid little needs,
His laboured breathing and the fretful way he cried
And longed for my wide range of interests again,
Whereas his mother sank without another care
To that dread level of nothing but life itself
And stayed day and night, till he was better, there.

Women may pretend, yet they always dismiss
Everything but mere being just like this.

*In reply to A. E. Housman's.

Bracken Hills in Autumn

These beds of bracken, climax of the summer's growth,
Are elemental as the sky or sea.
In still and sunny weather they give back
The sun's glare with a fixed intensity
      As of steel or glass
      No other foliage has.

There is a menace in their indifference to man
As in tropical abundance. On gloomy days
They redouble the sombre heaviness of the sky
And nurse the thunder. Their dense growth shuts the narrow
                                  ways
      Between the hills and draws
      Closer the wide valleys' jaws.

This flinty verdure's vast effusion is the more
Remarkable for the shortness of its stay.
From November to May a brown stain on the slopes
Downbeaten by frost and rain, then in quick array
      The silvery crooks appear
      And the whole host is here.

Useless they may seem to men and go unused, but cast
Cartloads of them into a pool where the trout are few
And soon the swarming animalculae upon them
Will proportionately increase the fishes too.
      Miracles are never far away
      Save bringing new thought to play.

In summer islanded in these grey-green seas where the wind
                                  plucks
The pale underside of the fronds on gusty days
As a land breeze stirs the white caps in a roadstead
Glimpses of shy bog gardens surprise the gaze
      Or rough stuff keeping a ring
      Round a struggling water-spring.

Look closely. Even now bog asphodel spikes, still alight at the
tips,
Sundew lifting white buds like those of the whitlow grass
On walls in spring over its little round leaves
Sparkling with gummy red hairs, and many a soft mass
Of the curious moss that can clean
A wound or poison a river, are seen.

Ah! well I know my tumultuous days now at their prime
Will be brief as the bracken too in their stay
Yet in them as the flowers of the hills 'mid the bracken
All that I treasure is needs hidden away
And will also be dead
When its rude cover is shed.

(from *New Saltire*, August 1962)

Third Hymn to Lenin

for Muriel Rukeyser

> *None can usurp this height (returned that shade)*
> *But those to whom the miseries of the world*
> *Are miseries, and will not let them rest.* KEATS *Hyperion*

These that have turned the world upside down are come hither also.
Acts *xvii*, 6.
*The night is far spent, the day is at hand, let us therefore cast off the works of
darkness, and let us put on the armour of light.* Romans *xiii*, 12.

Glasgow is a city of the sea, but what avails
In this great human Sargasso even that flair,
That resolution to understand all bearings
That is the essence of a seaman's character,
The fruit of first-hand education in the ways of ships,
The ways of man, and the ways of women even more,
Since these resemble sea and weather most
And are the deepest source of all appropriate lore.

A cloud no bigger than a man's hand, a new
Note in the wind, an allusion over the salt-junk,

And seamen are aware of "a number of things",
That sense of concealed but powerful meanings sunk
In hints that almost pass too quick to seize,
Which must be won out of the abysses
Above and below, is second nature to them
But not enough in such a sink as this is.

What seaman in the history of the world before
On such an ocean as you sailed could say
This wave will recede, this advance, knew every wave
By name, and foresaw its inevitable way
And the final disposition of the whirling whole;
So identified at every point with the historic flow
That, even as you pronounced, so it occurred?
You turned a whole world right side up, and did so
With no dramatic gesture, no memorable word.
Now measure Glasgow for a like laconic overthrow!

On days of revolutionary turning points you literally
      flourished,
Became clairvoyant, foresaw the movement of classes,
And the probable zig-zags of the revolution
As if on your palm;
Not only an analytical mind but also
A great constructive, synthesizing mind
Able to build up in thought the new reality
As it must actually come
By force of definite laws eventually,
Taking into consideration, of course,
Conscious interference, the bitter struggle
For the tasks still before the Party, and the class it leads
As well as possible diversions and inevitable actions
Of all other classes. – Such clairvoyance is the result
Of a profound and all-sided knowledge of life
With all its richness of colour, connexions and relations.
Hence the logic of your speeches – "like some all-powerful
      feelers
Economic, political, ideological, and so forth.

Which grasp, once for all, all sides as in a vise,
And one has no strength left to tear away from their
    embrace;
Either one yields or decides upon complete failure."

As some great seaman or some poet grasps
The practical meaning, ideal beauty, traditional fascination,
Intellectual importance and emotional chances combined
In any instant in his particular situation,
So here there is a like accumulation of effects,
On countless planes of significance at once,
And all we see is set in riddling terms,
Making aught but myriad-mindedness a dunce.

How can the points be taken quickly enough,
Meaning behind meaning, dense forests of cross-reference;
How can the wood be seen for such a chaos of trees;
How from the hydra's mouths glean any sense?
The logic and transitions of the moment taken,
On the spur of the moment all the sheer surface
And rapid narrative "the public wants" secured,
How grasp the "darker purposes" and win controlling
    place?

We are but fools who live by headlines else,
Surfriders merely of the day's sensations,
Living in the flicker like a cinema fan,
Nor much dedoped, defooled, by any patience.
Mere Study's fingers cannot grasp the roots of power.
Be with me, Lenin, reincarnate in me here,
Fathom and solve as you did Russia erst
This lesser maze, you greatest proletarian seer!

Hard test, my master, for another reason.
The whole of Russia had no Hell like this.*
There is no place in all the white man's world
So sunk in the unspeakable abyss.
            *i.e. the slums of Glasgow.

Only a country whose chief glory is the Kirk,
A country with our fetish of efficiency and thrift,
With endless loving sentiment to mask the facts,
Has such an infernal masterpiece in its gift.

A horror that might sicken your stomach even,
The peak of the capitalist system and the trough of Hell,
Fit testimonial to our ultra-pious race,
A people greedy, lying, and unconscionable
Beyond compare. – Seize on this link, spirit of Lenin, then
And you must needs haul upwards to the light
The whole base chain of the phenomena that hold
Europe so far below levels worthy of its might!

Do you know the haunting slum smell? Do you remember
Proust's account of a urinal's dark-green and yellow scent,
Or Gillies' remark when Abelard complained
Of Guibert's horrible cooking, worse than excrement,
Yet he had watched him scour the crocks himself:
"He never washes the cloth he scrubs them with.
That gives the taste, the odour; the world's worst yet."
But no! We've progressed. Words fail for this all-
      pervasive
Slum stench. A corpse beside it is a violet.

"*Door after door as we knocked was opened by a shirted
man, suddenly and softly as if impelled forward by the over-
powering smell behind him. It is this smell which is the most
oppressive symbol of such lives; choking, nauseating; the smell
of corrupt sweat and unnamed filthiness of body. That smell!
Sometimes it crept out at us past the legs of the householder,
insinuatingly, as if ashamed; sometimes it brazened out foul
and pestiferous. Once in a woman's shilling boarding-house it
leapt out and took us by the throat like an evil beast. The
smell of the slums, the unforgettable, the abominable smell!*" –
BOLITHO: *The Cancer of Empire*, describing the slums of
Glasgow.*

Ah, lizard eyes, how I would love to see
You reincarnate here and taking issue
With the piffling spirits of our public men,
Going through them like a machine-gun through crinkled
    tissue,
But first of all – in Cranston's tea-rooms* say –
With some of our leading wart-hogs calmly sat
Watching the creatures' sardonically toothsome faces
Die out in horror like Alice's Cheshire cat.

We, who have seen the daemons one by one
Emerging in the modern world and know full well
Our rapport with the physical world is safe
So long as we avoid all else and dwell,
Heedless of the multiplicity of correspondences
Behind them, on the simple data our normal senses give,
Know what vast liberating powers these dark powers
    disengage,
But leave the task to others and in craven safety live.

Normal, thanks to the determined blindness we possess
To all that might upset our little apple-carts,
Too cautious to do anything about it,
Knowing our days are brief, though these slum parts
Harbour hosts of larves, legions of octopuses,
Pulsing in the dark air, with the wills and powers
To rise in scaly depravity to unthinkable heights
And annihilate forever all that is ours.

And only here and there a freak like me
Looking at himself, all of him, with intensest scrutiny,
See how he runs round like a dog, every particle
Concentrated on getting in safe somewhere, while he
With equal determination must push himself out,
Feel more at all costs, experience more, be shattered more,
Driven towards an unqualifiable upward and onward
That is – all morons feel – suicidally over the score.

*Well-known Glasgow restaurant, former resort of Glasgow Labour
M.P.s and leading supporters.

Our frantic efforts go all ways and go none;
Incontinent with vain hopes, tireless Micawbers,
Banking on what Gladstone said in 1890
Or Christ a few centuries earlier, – there's
No lack of counsellors, of *die List der Vernunft*.
The way to Hell is paved with plenty of talk,
But nothing ever happens – nothing ever will;
The future's always rosy, the present no less black.

Clever – and yet we cannot solve this problem even;
Civilised – and flaunting such a monstrous sore;
Christian – in flat defiance of all Christ taught;
Proud of our country with this open sewer at our door,
Come, let us shed all this transparent bluff,
Acknowledge our impotence, the prize eunuchs of Europe,
Battening on our shame, and with voices weak as bats'
Proclaiming in ghoulish kirks our base immortal hope.

And what is this impossible problem then?
Only to give a few thousand people enough to eat,
Decent houses and a fair income every week.
What? For nothing? Yes! Scotland can well afford it.

It cannot be done. The poor are always with us,
The Bible says. Would other countries agree?
Clearly we couldn't unless they did it too.
All the old arguments against ending Slavery!

Ah, no! These bourgeois hopes are not our aim.

Lenin, lover of music, who dare not listen to it,
Teach us to eschew all the siren voices too
And get due *Diesseitigkeit*. Countless petty indulgences
– We give them fine names, like Culture, it is true –
Lure us up this enchanting side-line and up that
When we should stay in stinking vennel and wynd,
Not masturbating our immortal souls,
But simply doing some honest service to mankind.

Great forces dedicated to the foulest ends
Are reaping a rich victory in Glasgow here
In life stunted and denied and endless misery,
Preventible disease and "crime" and death; and standing
    sheer
Behind these crowded thoroughfares with armaments
    concealed
Ready at any vital move to massacre
These mindless mobs, the gangsters lurk, the officer class,
    ruthless
Watching Glasgow's every step and lusting to attack her.

And freedom's opposing forces are hidden too,
But Fascism has its secret agents everywhere
In every coward's castle, shop, bank, manse and school
While few serve Freedom's counter-service there,
Nor can they serve – for all but all men's ears
Are deaf to aught it says, stuffed with the wax
Of ignorant prejudice and subsidised inanity
Till Freedom to their minds all access lacks.

And most insidious and stultifying of all
The anti-human forces have instilled the thought
That knowledge has outrun the individual brain
Till trifling details only can be brought
Within the scope of any man; and so have turned
Humanity's vast achievements against the human mind
Until a sense of general impotence compels
Most men in petty grooves to stay confined.

This is the lie of lies – the High Treason to mankind.
No one but fritters half his time away.
It is the human instinct – the will to use it – that's destroyed
Till only one or two in every million men today
Know that thought is reality – and thought alone! –
And must absorb all the material – their goal
The mastery by the spirit of all the facts that can be known.

Instead of that we have a Jeans accommodating the stars
To traditional superstitions, and a Barnes who thrids
Divers geometries – Euclidean, Lobatchewskyan,
    Riemannian –
And Cepheid variables, white dwarfs, yet stubbornly
    heads
(Though he admits his futile journey fails to reach
Any solution of the problem of "God's" relation to Time)
Back to his starting place – to a like betrayal
Of the scientific spirit to a dud Sublime.

And in Scotland a Haldane even, rendering great service
    to biological theory
In persistently calling attention to the special form of
    organization
Existing in living things – yet failing greatly
Through his defeatist wish to accept
This principle of organization as axiomatic
Instead of tracing its relation to the lower principle of
    organization
Seen in paracrystals, colloids, and so forth.
Threading with great skill the intricate shuttling path
From "spontaneity" to preoccupation with design,
From the realistic "moment" to the abstraction of essential
    form
And ending with a fusion of all their elements,
At once realistic and abstract,

   "*Daring and unblushing atheism is creeping abroad and
saturating the working population, which are the proper persons
to be saturated with it. I look to no others. It has been said to
me by more than one person, 'Let us write in the style of Hume
and Gibbon and seek readers among the higher classes.' I
answer 'No'; I know nothing of the so-called higher classes
but that they are robbers; I will work towards the raising of
the working population above them.*" – RICHARD CARLILE

Or like Michael Roberts whose *New Country*
Is the same old country, and mediaeval enough his
    "modern mind"
Confessing that after all he cannot see
How civilization can be saved unless confined
Under the authority of a Church which in the West
Can only be the so-called Christian Church.
Perish the thought! Let us take our stand
Not on this infernal old parrot's perch
But squarely with Richard Carlile: "The enemy with
    whom we have to grapple
Is one with whom no peace can be made. Idolatry will not
    parley,
Superstition will not treat or covenant. They must be
    uprooted
Completely for public and individual safety."

Michael Roberts and All Angels! Auden, Spender, those
    bhoyos,
All yellow twicers: not one of them
With a tithe of Carlile's courage and integrity.
Unlike these pseudos I am *of* – not *for* – the working class
And like Carlile know nothing of the so-called higher
    classes
Save only that they are cheats and murderers,
Battening like vampires on the masses.

The illiteracy of the literate! But Glasgow's hordes
Are not even literate save a man or two;
All bogged in words that communicate no thought,
Only mumbo-jumbo, fraudulent clap-trap, ballyhoo.
The idiom of which constructive thought avails itself
Is unintelligible save to a small minority
And all the rest wallow in exploded fallacies
And cherish for immortal souls their gross stupidity,
While in the deeper layers of their ignorance who delves
Finds in this order – Scotland, other men, themselves.
We do not play or keep any mere game's conventions.

Our concern is human wholeness – the child-like spirit
Newborn every day – not, indeed, as careless of tradition
Nor of the lessons of the past: these it must needs inherit.

But as capable of such complete assimilation and surrender,
So all-inclusive, unfenced-off, uncategoried, sensitive and
      tender,
That growth is unconditioned and unwarped – Ah, Lenin,
Life and that more abundantly, thou Fire of Freedom,
Fire-like in your purity and heaven-seeking vehemence,
Yet the adjective must not suggest merely meteoric,
Spectacular – not the flying sparks but the intense
Glowing core of your character, your large and splendid
      stability
Made you the man you were – the live heart of all
      humanity!

Spirit of Lenin, light on this city now!

Light up this city now!

            (from *Three Hymns to Lenin*, 1957)

Island Funeral

The procession winds like a little snake
Between the walls of irregular grey stones
Piled carelessly on one another.
Sometimes, on this winding track,
The leaders are doubled back
Quite near to us.

It is a grey world, sea and sky
Are colourless as the grey stones,
And the small fields are hidden by the walls
That fence them on every side.

Seen in perspective, the walls
Overlap each other
As far as the skyline on the hill,
Hiding every blade of grass between them,
So that all the island appears
One jumble of grey boulders.
The last grey wall outlined on the sky
Has the traceried effect
Of a hedge of thorns in winter.

The men in the stiff material
Of their homespun clothes
Look like figures cut from cardboard,
But shod in their rawhide rivelins
They walk with the springing step of mountaineers.
The women wear black shawls,
And black or crimson skirts.

A line of tawny seaweed fringes the bay
Between high-water mark and low.
It is luminous between the grey of rocky shore
And the grey of sullen water.

We can now and then look over a wall
Into some tiny field. Many of these
Are nothing but grey slabs of limestone,
Smooth as any pavement,
With a few blades of grass
Struggling up through the fissures,
And the grey surface of that rock
Catches and holds the light
As if it was water lying there.

At last the long line halts and breaks up,
And, like a stream flowing into a loch,
The crowd pours from the narrow lane
Into the cemetery where on an unfenced sandhill
The grey memorial stones of the island
Have no distinction from the country.

The coffin lies tilted a little sideways
On the dark grey sand flung up from the grave.

A little priest arrives; he has a long body and short legs
And wears bicycle clips on his trousers.
He stands at the head of the grave
And casts a narrow purple ribbon round his neck
And begins without delay to read the Latin prayers
As if they were a string of beads.
Twice the dead woman's son hands him a bottle
And twice he sprinkles the coffin and the grave
With holy water. In all the faces gathered round
There is a strange remoteness.
They are weather-beaten people with eyes grown clear,
Like the eyes of travellers and seamen,
From always watching far horizons.
But there is another legend written on these faces,
A shadow – or a light – of spiritual vision
That will seldom find full play
On the features of country folk
Or men of strenuous action.
Among these mourners are believers and unbelievers,
And many of them steer a middle course,
Being now priest-ridden by convention
And pagan by conviction,
But not one of them betrays a sign
Of facile and self-lulling piety,
Nor can one see on any face
"A sure and certain hope
Of the Resurrection to eternal life."
This burial is just an act of nature,
A reassertion of the islanders' inborn certainty
That "in the midst of life we are in death."
It is unlike the appointed funerals of the mainland
With their bitter pageantry
And the ramp of undertakers and insurance companies
That makes death seem incredible and cruel.
There are no loafing onlookers.

Everyone is immediately concerned
In what is taking place.
All through their lives death has been very close to them,
And this funeral of one who had been "a grand woman"
Seems to be but a reminder
Of the close comradeship between living and dying.

Down in the bay there is a row of curraghs
Drawn up on the sand. They lie keel upwards,
Each one shining black and smooth
Like some great monster of the sea,
Symbols to the island folk of their age-long
Battle with the waves, a battle where in daily life
The men face death and the women widowhood.

Four men fill in the grave with dark grey sand,
Then they cover the sand
With green sods and rough-hewn boulders,
And finally an old man with a yellow beard
Helps the four young gravediggers
In levering a great slab of stone
Until it lies flat upon the grave,
And the people watch all this in silence.
Then the crowd scatters east and west
And, last, the four gravediggers,
All of them laughing now
With the merriment of clowns.
There are few and fewer people
On the island nowadays,
And there are more ruins of old cottages
Than occupied homes.
I love to go into these little houses
And see and touch the pieces of furniture.
I know all there is to know
About their traditional plenishing
And native arts and crafts,
And can speak with authority
About tongue-and-groove cleats,

The lipped drawer, and the diameters of finials.
But I know them also in their origin
Which is the Gaelic way of life
And can speak with equal authority
About a people one of whose proverbs
Is the remarkable sentence:
"Every force evolves a form."
While this thing lasted
It was pure and very strong.
In an old island room the sense is still strong
Of being above and beyond the familiar,
The world as we know it,
In an atmosphere purified,
As it were, from the non-essentials of living
– An intangible feeling,
Difficult to describe,
But easy to recall to anyone
Who has stood in such a room
And been disturbed by the certainty
That those who once inhabited it
Were sure of every thought they had.

To enter almost any of the island rooms even today
Is to be profoundly conscious of this emanation,
At once so soothing and so strangely agitating.
Fifty years ago a visitor wrote: "They are there to stay,
And that fact accounts for a great deal.
It is partial explanation of the contentment
On the faces of the island women.
It is a reason for the repose and settledness
Which pervade an island village
– That indefinable something,
So altogether unlike the life of ordinary villages,
And which you feel in the air,
And are conscious of by some instinct, as men claim
To be aware of the presence of spirits.
There is no restlessness,
Or fret of business,

Or anxiety about anything.
It is as if the work was done,
And it was one eternal afternoon."
But they have not, in fact, stayed,
Foully forced out by their inferiors –
Red-faced, merely physical people
Whose only thought looking over
These incomparable landscapes
Is what sport they will yield
– How many deer and grouse.
The old stock are few and ever fewer now.
But they expected to stay,
And they deserved to stay,
Just as they expected there would always be
Thousands of them to work incessantly and serenely
At the making of objects which said:
"There is great beauty in harmony."
They lived as much like one another as possible,
And they kept as free as they could of the world at large.
It is not their creed as such, however,
That explains them and the beauty of their work.

It is rather the happiness with which they held it,
The light-heartedness with which they enslaved themselves
To the various rituals it demanded,
And also the circumstance that they were all
Poor people – whose notions of form
Were both ancient and basic.
They began with the barest patterns, the purest beginnings
Of design, in their minds, and then
Something converted them into artists
With an exalted lyric gift.
What that something was
No one can claim perfectly to know.
Some of them were reported as believing
In assistance from the angels.
Whatever the source, the result was some
Of the most beautiful work the world has ever seen.

And even now, in Edinburgh or Glasgow or London,
I often move my ear up close
The better to distinguish in the raucous mixture
The sound of the cornet I want to hear,
And you may see my face light up
With recognition and appreciation at various points,
And hear me comment, "The greatest of them all."
The term is justified – this island note,
This clear old Gaelic sound,
In the chaos of the modern world,
Is like a phrase from Beiderbecke's cornet,
As beautiful as any phrase can be.
It is, in its loveliness and perfection,
Unique, as a phrase should be;
And it is ultimately indescribable.

Panassié speaks of it as "full and powerful",
But also as "so fine
As to be almost transparent,"
And there is in fact
This extraordinary delicacy in strength.
He speaks of phrases that soar;
And this, too, is in fact
A remarkable and distinguishing quality.
Otis Ferguson speaks of "the clear line
Of that music," of "every phrase
As fresh and glistening as creation itself",
And there is in fact
This radiance, and simple joyousness.
These terms tell a great deal, but there remains
Much that eludes words completely
And can only be heard.
And though one can account for the music
Up to a certain point by the quality of the person
– The "candour, force, personal soundness, good humour" –
There have been other people – and still are, no doubt –
With candour, force, personal soundness and good humour
And one has still to explain, as always,

How these qualities translated themselves
In this instance into such musical phrases.
In the din of our modern world
The Gaelic spirit plays merely
As an unfeatured member of well-known bands
– Which means that one hears it sometimes – very rarely! –
For a full chorus, sometimes merely for a phrase,
Sometimes only in the background with the rest of the brass.
But even the phrase detaches itself from its surroundings
As something exquisite and perfect; and even playing
Along with the others in the background
It stands out from them,
Not through any aggressiveness but solely
Through the distinctive quality of its style.
"The greatest of them all" – but
There is little life left on the island now,
And soon the last funeral
Will take place there,
And in the rowdy chaos of the world
The sound of this cornet will be heard no more
– One will listen and one's face will never
Light up with recognition and appreciation again.

Yet if the nature of the mind is determined
By that of the body, as I believe,
It follows that every type of human mind
Has existed an infinite number of times
And will do so. Materialism promises something
Hardly to be distinguished from eternal life.
Minds or souls with the properties I love
– The minds or souls of these old islanders –
Have existed during an eternal time in the past
And will exist for an eternal time in the future.
A time broken up of course
By enormous intervals of non-existence,
But an infinite time.
If one regards these personalities
As possessing some value

There is a certain satisfaction
In the thought that in eternity
They will be able to develop
In all possible environments
And to express themselves
In all the ways possible to them
– A logical deduction from thoroughgoing Materialism
And independent of the precise type
Of materialism developed.
It is quite unimportant whether we call
Our ultimate reality matter, electric charge,
Ψ-waves, mind-stuff, neural stuff, or what not,
Provided it obeys laws which can, in principle,
Be formulated mathematically.

The cornet solo of our Gaelic islands
Will sound out every now and again
Through all eternity.

I have heard it and am content for ever.

(from *The Islands of Scotland*, 1939)

Facing the Chair

Here under the radiant rays of the sun
Where everything grows so vividly
In the human mind and in the heart,
Love, life, and all else so beautifully,
I think again of men as innocent as I am
Pent in a cold unjust walk between steel bars,
Their trousers slit for the electrodes
And their hair cut for the cap

Because of the unconcern of men and women,
Respectable and respected and professedly Christian,
Idle-busy among the flowers of their gardens here
Under the gay-tipped rays of the sun,

And I am suddenly completely bereft
Of *la grande amitié des choses crées*,
The unity of life which can only be forged by love.

(from the *Scotsman*, 9 November 1968)

Crystals Like Blood

I remember how, long ago, I found
Crystals like blood in a broken stone.

I picked up a broken chunk of bed-rock
And turned it this way and that,
It was heavier than one would have expected
From its size. One face was caked
With brown limestone. But the rest
Was a hard greenish-grey quartz-like stone
Faintly dappled with darker shadows,
And in this quartz ran veins and beads
Of bright magenta.

And I remember how later on I saw
How mercury is extracted from cinnabar
– The double ring of iron piledrivers
Like the multiple legs of a fantastically symmetrical spider
Rising and falling with monotonous precision,
Marching round in an endless circle
And pounding up and down with a tireless, thunderous force,
While, beyond, another conveyor drew the crumbled ore
From the bottom and raised it to an opening high
In the side of a gigantic grey-white kiln.

So I remember how mercury is got
When I contrast my living memory of you
And your dear body rotting here in the clay
– And I feel once again released in me
The bright torrents of felicity, naturalness, and faith
My treadmill memory draws from you yet.

(from *Poetry Scotland*, 1949)

from

IN MEMORIAM JAMES JOYCE
(1955)

To distinctly English writers in England
Authenticity is never allowed;
The quality is perhaps
Not even known to exist.
There are too many vested interests.
In the United States Mark Twain
Could finally make headway
Against the Transcendentalists;
Poe could stand with his body starved
But his mind making its mark.
He had to fight many battles
Against many unscrupulous cliques,
And in the end his head became
Both bloody and bowed
But neither he, alive
Nor his reputation, he dead,
Have had to contend with the dead weight
Of dead, vested interests
And merely political disingenuousnesses
That have strangled
Most literary brightnesses
In England for a hundred years.
These tendencies work
Towards a wilderness of thumbs down.
It was Landor who first said
That every Frenchman takes a personal share
In the glory of his poets
Whereas every Englishman resents
The achievements of his poets
Because they detract
From the success of his own "poetry";
And the remark was extraordinarily profound.
So the English literary world

Is an immense arena
Where every spectator is intent
On the deaths of those awaiting judgement
And every gladiator is intent
On causing the death of his fellow-combatant
By smiting him with the corpses
Of others predeceased.
The method, the mania, the typical
"Fair-play" of "the sporting English"
Is really extraordinary in its operation.

Supposing, having no pet author of your own
Out of whose entrails
You hope to make a living,
No political bias,
No interest in a firm of publishers
Who make dividends out of other "classics",
You timidly venture to remark
That Trollope, Jane Austen,
And the Mrs Gaskell of *Mary Barton*,
Are English Authors
Authentic in their methods.

"*But*" you hear the professional reviewers
All protesting at once
"Trollope has not the humour of Dickens,
The irony of Thackeray,
The skill with a plot of Wilkie Collins.
Jane Austen has not the wit of Meredith,
The reforming energy of Charles Reade,
The imperial sense of Charles Kingsley,
The tender pathos of the author of *Cranford*.
And as for Mrs Gaskell who wrote *Cranford*,
Well, she has not the aloofness of Jane Austen,
And Christina Rossetti had not
The manly optimism of Browning,
And Browning lacked the religious confidence
Of Christina Rossetti, or the serenity

Of Matthew Arnold. And who was Matthew Arnold?
Landor could not write about whist and old playbills
Like Charles Lamb.
(*Saint Charles, Thackeray murmured softly!*)

No one who has paid any attention at all
To official-critical appraisements of English writers
Can gainsay the moral to be drawn
From these instances of depreciation
Or the truth of the projection itself.
Literary figures should, of course,
As is said of race-horses, be "tried high,"
But to attach a Derby winner to a stone cart,
And then condemn it as a horse
Because it does not make so much progress
As a Clydesdale or a Percheron
Is to try the animal
Altogether too high.
And not fairly.

English official criticism has erected
A stone-heap, a dead load of moral qualities.
A writer must have optimism, irony,
A healthy outlook,
A middle-class standard of morality,
As much religion as, say, St Paul had,
As much atheism as Shelley had . . .
And, finally, on top of an immense load
Of self-neutralising moral and social qualities,
Above all, Circumspection,
So that, in the end, no English writer
According to these standards,
Can possess authenticity.
The formula is this: Thackeray is not Dickens,
So Thackeray does not represent English literature.
Dickens is not Thackeray, *so he*
Does not represent English literature.
In the end literature itself is given up

And you have the singular dictum
Of the doyen of English official literary criticism.
This gentleman writes ... but always rather uncomfortably ...
Of Dryden as divine, of Pope as divine,
Of Swift as so filthy
As to intimidate the self-respecting critic.
But when he comes to Pepys of course
His enthusiasm is unbounded.
He salutes the little pawky diarist
With an affection, an enthusiasm,
For his industry, his pawkiness,
His thumb-nail sketches.
Then he asserts amazingly:
"This is scarcely literature"
And continues with panegyrics that leave no doubt
That the critic considers the Diary
To be something very much better.
The judgement is typically English.
The bewildered foreigner can only say:
"But if the Diary is all you assert of it,
It must be literature, or, if it is not literature,
It cannot be all you assert of it."
And obviously ...

I once met a Peruvian who had come
To London to study English literature.
He said: "Oh! but your writers, they pant and they pant;
Producing and producing! And then, as the type,
The Arch-type, you have ...
Charles Lamb *On Buttered Toast!*"
I said: "Ah! That is because
You are not an Englishman!"

Some other books published by Penguins are described on the following pages.

THE PENGUIN BOOK OF SCOTTISH VERSE

Edited by Tom Scott

This anthology begins with an anonymous poem of the late thirteenth century. However, the history of Scottish poetry goes back much further. As with that of the Irish, it has Gaelic origins. Moreover Scottish literature is written in no less than five languages.

The Penguin Book of Scottish Verse contains only a small, but enticing, section of the poetry which may be claimed as Scottish in the widest sense. It is a selection of poems written in Scots and English, or an amalgam of both, dating from about the 1300s to the present day. To help the general reader unfamiliar with Scottish orthography, the editor has added useful footnotes where necessary, and has tried to standardize the Scots of the pre-Reformation writers without forfeiting the integrity of the poems.

THE PENGUIN BOOK OF SCOTTISH
SHORT STORIES

Edited by J. F. Hendry

These twenty stories present a composite picture of the various facets of Scottish writing today. The best of Scottish writing is no mere brew of mists, tartans, and the macabre, but clear, objective, and realistic in spirit: these stories have therefore been selected on a broad basis, without any requirement that they deal with the 'Scottish scene'. By striking a balance between older and younger writers and between stories with a Scottish setting and others (which are no less traditional) the editor has achieved an interesting collection of names as well known as Linklater, Mitchison, and Spark and names which deserve to be better known. One thing is certain: these writers are all Scots.